I0456422

Twelve Essentials For a Successful Marriage

DR. LLOYD SLOWE

Twelve Essentials For a Successful Marriage
Copyright © 2024 by Dr. Lloyd Slowe

All rights reserved. No part of this publication may be reproduced, distributed, or transmitted in any form or by any means, including photocopying, recording, or other electronic or mechanical methods, without the prior written permission of the author, except in the case of brief quotations embodied in critical reviews and certain other non-commercial uses permitted by copyright law.

Library of Congress Control Number: 2024919338

ISBN
978-1-964488-29-5 (Paperback)
978-1-964488-30-1 (eBook)
978-1-964488-28-8 (Hardcover)

The book that you are about to read was designed to facilitate the entire core of a family. It is comprehensive in terms of information which will guide you into all truths. The context of this book is intended to reach the desired needs of young people who are currently courting, engaged couples who are in preparation to say "I do", couples who are currently struggling in their marriages, and are seeking workable solutions, and couples who are on the verge of divorce. It is a holistic and unprecedented approach for premarital and post-marital couples all around the world.

Thank God for his ingenious inspiration, which caused my passion for this subject to emerge from a thought to a book. I also want to recognize my wife, and thank her for her tireless efforts of support in supporting me every step of the way.

Thanks to my professor, Dr. Ronald Smith, for his embrace and cheerleader role, which he displayed by giving his support and encouragement to put this book together.

And to all of my readers, this is from my heart to yours.

Table of Contents

PREFACE

Twelve Essentials for a Successful Marriage

I count this an honor and a privilege to get out of my comfort zone and use my pen and pad to articulate one of the most interesting yet controversial subjects in life (from the biblical perspective). One would expect that since the union between a man and a woman was originated or instituted by God Almighty, divorce would not be so prevalent, especially among believers or the Church. We, however, need to study the text taken from Mark 10:9 in the biblical quote, "therefore, what God has joined together, let no one separate."

First of all, please understand that God didn't join every man and woman who is married. For what God joined, no one can disjoin. People join themselves for several reasons, most of which are wrong and evil, and God has no part in such unions. Money can't keep your marriage together, sex can't keep your marriage together, nor can material possessions keep your marriage together. The common denominator that will keep your marriage together is the love of God, or God's love (agape). He is the author of the book that talks about marriage, and gives detailed counseling regarding the subject. For this reason, you have to trust him with your relationships. He is the master builder. He knows what needs fixing, what to fix, where to fix it, how to fix it, and why.

I'm proud to announce that I have been married for twenty-seven years, and thanks be to God, he has been sustaining our union on a daily basis. In spite of the challenges we face every day, we have learned how to appreciate, acknowledge, and praise God every day of our lives. My wife and I apply 2 Corinthians 13 in our relationship in spite of what's happening in the world. Remember that variety is the spice of life. Apply variety in your dressing, eating, looking, giving, and praying. May God bless and inspire you as you read this book.

1

Definition And Etymology Of Marriage

When two people are under the influence of the most violent, most insane, deceptive, and most transient of passions, they are required to pledge that they will remain in that excited, abnormal, and exhausting condition until death do they part.

Divine purposes in marriage: The first man and woman God created were Adam and Eve, who became the first couple. God himself officiated at their wedding, which marked the beginning not only of their union, but also of the institution of marriage. Genesis 2:21–24 says: "And the Lord God caused a deep sleep to fall upon Adam, and he slept: and he took one of his ribs, and closed up the flesh instead thereof, and the rib, which the Lord God had taken from man, made he woman, and brought her to the man. And Adam said, "This is now bone of my bones, and flesh of my flesh; she shall be called Woman, because she was taken out of Man." Therefore shall a man leave his father and mother, and shall cleave unto his wife: and they shall be one flesh."

Through the institution of marriage, God sought to achieve two purposes:

1) He wanted man to have the experience of complete human love. Genesis 2:18–20 says, "And the Lord said, It is not good that the man should be alone; I will make him a helper comparable to him. And out of the ground the Lord God formed every beast of the field, and every fowl of the air, and brought them unto Adam to see what he would call them: And whatsoever Adam called every living creature that was the name thereof. And Adam gave names to all cattle and to the fowl of the air and to every beast of the field; but for Adam there was not found a helper comparable to him."

2) The love between a man and his wife is a physical love, for "they shall be one flesh" (Gen. 2:24) yet it is also an emotional love, for the man "shall cleave unto his wife." That is, he will hold her warmly without ever letting her go. And their love is also friendship, for she will be his constant helper (Gen. 2:18)—always present or available.

A perfect love between husbands and wives mirrors God's love for the Church (see Ephesians 5:21–33) "submitting to one another in the fear of God. Wives, submit to your own husband, as to the Lord. For the husband is the head of the wife, as also Christ the head of the church; and he is the Savior of the body. Therefore, just as the church is subject to Christ, so let the wives be to their own husbands in everything. Husbands, love your wives, just as Christ also loved the church and gave himself for her, that he might sanctify and cleanse her with the washing of water by the word. That he might present her to himself a glorious church, not having spot or wrinkle or any such thing, but that she should be holy and without blemish. So husbands ought to love their own wives as their own bodies; he who loves his wife loves himself. For no one ever hated his own flesh, but nourishes and cherishes it, just as the Lord does the church; for we are members of his body, of his flesh, and of his bones. "For this reason a man shall leave his father and mother and be joined to his wife, and the two shall be come one flesh." This may be difficult to understand, but I speak concerning Christ and the church. Nevertheless let each one of you in particular so love his own wife as himself, and let the wife see that she respects her husband."

We are living in a changing, modern society that is willing to give their intimate relationships (marriage) a trial, rather than approach them with a nonreversible covenant in mind, which is God's way. Many have lured themselves into a prenuptial agreement, which is a contract entered into by two people prior to marriage or civil union. The content of a prenuptial agreement can vary widely, but commonly includes provisions for the division of property and specifies what each person's property rights will be, should the couple divorce, and any rights to spousal support during or after the dissolution of marriage.

Prenuptial agreements can bring on a constant suspicion to the relationship, and create attitudes that are not submissive based upon God's word and God's intention for marriage. Prenuptial agreements take away the very essence of love and tranquility from the relationship. It brings you as a couple into bondage, and places limits over your life. It is saying, "If you only cross the line one more time, that's it, for our relationship." Don't go here, don't go there, or don't do this, do that. You will literally fill your spouse's life with do's and the dont's…all because of the consequences that are behind those controlling and devious "do's and dont's".

Every marriage that is directed by the Holy Spirit should build on the foundation of love. Let me clarify the first sentence in this paragraph, because there are those who believe that the Holy Spirit directs all marriages. That is wrong. People marry for several reasons. Some people do it for the money. In my opinion, Anna Nicole Smith was one of them. She married ninety-four-year-old J. Howard Marshall, an oil tycoon, who was worth was approximately $1.6 billion in his estate. There are many other celebrities who marry for wealth and fame.

Other folks marry for property, for looks, for sex, for convenience; some marry because their biological clocks are ticking, others for immigration status and so on…

The above ways and reasons for being married aren't built on the foundation of love, but rather on the foundation that you are not sure what you are going into. If love starts it, love should end it. Intimacy between a man and a woman should be for keeps and not a trial or tryout for a period of time to see if it will work or not. This is what prenuptial agreement is all about. God never intended for marriage to be a trial, but for it to be an everlasting relationship that has meaning, and is in compliance with God's word. At a wedding, in the company of witnesses, and the presence of God, the minister asks the bride and groom the same questions: "Will you, (groom's full name) take (bride's full name) to be your lawfully wedded wife? Will you love and comfort her, honor and keep her and, in joy and in sorrow, preserve with her this bond, holy and unbroken, until the coming the Lord Jesus Christ, or as long as you both live?" They should both respond with an emphatic *yes*.

That yes represents a covenant between the wife and husband that shouldn't be established on a tryout, which is subject to failure, but on a love which shall never fail. For 1 Corinthians 13:8 says, "Love never fails. But whether there are prophecies, they will fail; whether there are tongues, they will cease; whether there is knowledge, it will vanish away."

2

Understanding the Covenant from God's Perspective

Cultural Context

Societies are built upon the family unit. In other words, families are the building blocks of a nation. A society is as strong as the integrity of the families that compose the society in which they live. The unity and values of families collectively affect, if not transform, societies and local cultures. United families tend to be more economically secure, their children are better disciplined and emotionally stable, they provide a caring environment for children and the elderly, and many conduct themselves in ways that reflect family ideals. Christian families function as teams that direct their combined resources to accomplish a shared vision.

Marriage is considered by Christians as a divine institution that was inaugurated by God. Today, Christian marriage is viewed in three ways:

first, as a threefold covenant among God, man, and woman; second, as a contract between the couple and the state; and third, as a pledge of faithfulness between the two (wife and husband who were married). The actual ceremony of Christian marriage is based on teachings in the Old Testament, but not in Jewish customs, except for Christians who live in cultures similar to those of ancient Israel. Messianic Jews often follow customs associated with ancient Jewish marriages.

The core precept of Christian marriage is the actual union of a man and woman who "become" united by God through a marriage covenant. In theology, this union is considered holy (set apart as consecrated) and representative of the perfect union among the Father, Son, and Holy Spirit. Two "become" one physically, spiritually, emotionally, economically, and socially. The process, through time, of "becoming" one is initiated at betrothal, celebrated in the ceremony, consummated in sexual union, and matured through the challenges of life.

Biblical Foundation

God established marriage in the beginning of human history when he created man (Adam) and woman (Eve) in the garden. The first marriage was based on promise and was monogamous (Gen. 2:24). God is seen as creating and presenting the woman to the man, an act that continues until today. The act of marriage consists of leaving, cleaving, and becoming one flesh. Marriage incorporates the concepts of independence from parents; commitment to a marriage partner; sexual union; and a growing, interdependent relationship. According to *The Marriage Covenant: A Biblical Study On Marriage, Divorce, And Remarriage*, "Human marriages are meant to be like God's marriage covenant to his people in purpose and permanence."

The Genesis 2:24 commandment was repeated by Jesus in Matthew 19:5 and Mark 10:7, 8 and later by the Apostle Paul in his letter to the Ephesians (5:31). Other biblical references to the marriage covenant are found in Exodus and Deuteronomy; the marriage of the prophet Hosea; the writings of Jeremiah, Ezekiel, and Isaiah; the teaching of Malachi; Proverbs; and in Romans and 1 Corinthians. In Malachi 2:14, the text states, "...though she is your companion and your wife by covenant." In many biblical texts, marriage is used as an analogy to illustrate God's unique relationship with his people or to characterize people who keep his law as faithful and those who break his law as adulterers (unfaithful). An understanding of covenant marriage is foundational to understanding God's love and his covenants.

Through the prophet Hosea's marriage to a prostitute, who was an unfaithful wife, God revealed himself as a compassionate, forgiving husband. In Jeremiah, God reminds Israel that he was their husband and even though they were unfaithful, he would establish a new covenant with them. God taught Israel through Jeremiah that marriage is a sacred covenant in which both partners must be faithful. Isaiah describes the final restoration of Israel in terms of a loving and forgiving husband who will restore his unfaithful wife. Malachi concludes the Old Testament by stating that God was the witness to the covenant between them and their wives (Mal. 2:13, 14). Marriage is a covenant to which God is a witness. A closer study reveals God's intervention to bless those who are faithful and to judge those who are unfaithful to covenant agreements.

In the New Testament (covenant), Jesus Christ is the sacrificial Lamb who takes away the sins of the world. Through his vicarious death, a New Covenant was established, not on law, but on grace (favor based on Christ's atonement). The Holy Spirit who was sent by God at Pentecost to confirm the resurrection of Jesus Christ and indwell believers reinforces the marriage covenant; the completion of the biblical Canon; the establishment of the church to provide encouragement and an environment for growth; and the transforming work of God to mature each marriage partner. In the New Testament, the Holy Spirit, the Third Person of the Godhead, indwells believers and is available to help the married couple. He becomes a part of the marriage team.

Historical Background

According to the Bible, marriage was considered sacred from the times of the early church, but the marriage ceremony wasn't practiced by churches until around the eleventh century. During the first centuries,

Christian marriages were conducted according to civil laws; however, ministers were often called upon to bless the union, which relays that traces of marriage rites emerged in the fourth century and detailed ceremonies were recorded in the ninth century. After Christianity began to spread in Western Europe, in the eleventh century, it became a practice to hold weddings near a church and later in the church to seek God's blessing for the union. By the twelfth century, most wedding ceremonies were conducted by ministers. It was at the Church that a Christian marriage, conducted by clergy in a ceremony, was determined to be necessary to be valid.

Most evangelical and Pentecostal denominations share a common interpretation of the nature of marriage and require clergy members to conduct marriage ceremonies. In some cultures, marriages may include three separate ceremonies, i.e., civil, by a mayor; custom, by a leader of a tribe; and ecclesiastical, before a church congregation. The concept of marriage as a covenant is not shared by all Christian denominations, as some still prefer to focus on the legal or "agreement" aspects of the union. Evangelicals and Pentecostals prefer to think of marriage as a sacred covenant. Some scholars have seen a relationship between the laws of Moses and covenant marriage.

Christian Marriage

Christian marriage is not just an agreement or contract it is also a covenant. In secular society, marriages are based on agreements or contracts that may include a no-fault clause for the dissolution of the marriage. Christian marriage should not be entered into without counsel and wisdom. Christians are encouraged to marry Christians and to understand that marriage is a divine institution, honored by God. This concept differs from those who believe marriage is only about meeting personal needs, self-fulfillment, self-development, security, convenience, or childbearing.

Marriage is used by the prophets like a mirror to reflect the grace of God and as a means to reveal the meaning of covenant. One aspect of this covenant is related to the image of God. According to the

Genesis account, man and woman were created in God's image, which among other attributes includes the capacity to commune with God and with each other. Other aspects of the image include human will, intelligence, language, and conscience. In marriage, the image of God is reflected in the "unity" and "love" between the husband and wife, how they raise children according to positive principles, and how they relate to others in love.

In Ecclesiastes 4:9-12, a statement is made about the union of man and woman that "A threefold cord is not easily broken." My mentor shared a discussion with a professional rope maker who said, "A rope made of three strands is the strongest because all strands touch, which necessitates agreement." The addition of more strands does not strengthen a rope, because the additional strands cannot "touch" each other. In times of stress, when one or two strands begin to fray, the third strand will keep the rope from breaking. This analogy is used by Christians to illustrate how God, as the third and preeminent member of the marriage covenant, protects and oversees the marriage.

Covenant

God is a covenant God and the Bible is a covenant book, and covenant is the philosophy, core value, or heart of a Christian marriage. The word "covenant" is believed to be derived from the Hebrew word "cutting," although the etymology is not conclusive; other commentary adds that the word means "a solemn agreement with binding force." Covenant is also used to denote "alliance." In the New Testament, covenant is translated "disposition," "will" (estate), or "testament." A covenant was often a treaty or agreement between individuals or people groups. Each party was expected to abide by certain predetermined conditions. In Israel, God was called upon to be a witness to covenants.

A covenant ceremony was usually concluded with an oath to each party and it was customary for a gift or testimony to be offered as a witness. Every covenant was confirmed by animal sacrifice (shedding of blood). After the animal was divided into two parts, the parties walked through the halves of the sacrifice. Some call this the "walk of death," but the writer prefers the "walk of life" into a new relationship. The significance of the sacrifice referred to the cost of covenant (testament of death), the seriousness and penalty for breaking the covenant, and an allusion to promise. Some Christians view the concept of sacrifice as representing the two parties who have, through symbolism, died to a former agreement and conditions in order to live. An agreement adds that covenants were "cut," and not "made" (Ps. 50:5). After the ceremony, the parties often shared a communal meal.

The concept of sacrifice is at the core of covenant. It was the cost of the new relationship. Covenants in the Old Testament were sealed with the blood of an animal sacrifice, which looked forward to the substitutionary death of Jesus Christ. Animals were sacrificed and the blood stood as a testimony of the seriousness of the covenant. Christian marriage imposes a cost on the husband, wife, and God, which is focused on the "cutting" of a sacrifice, referring to the atonement of Jesus Christ. The concept of a wedding covenant conveys the idea that the two partners will no longer live independent lives, but will be interdependent and "one" in their relationship.

Role of Women

Women in a covenant marriage are considered equal to men, but unique in their roles as mothers, homemakers, or working professionals. Global cultures impact the roles of women and their status in the home; however, the Bible teaches equality between the sexes before God. The woman is considered the "weaker" sex, but not "lesser." Both the man and woman are loved equally by God and are objects of his love. Examples of great women of God are recorded throughout the Bible, i.e., Eve, Sarah, Deborah, Esther, Ruth, Pricilla, and Mary. God often calls women to accomplish divine purposes, which sometimes include leading men.

In a covenant marriage, each partner pledges his or her love, faithfulness, and trust to the other. The wife usually pledges her submission to her husband as the prophet, priest, and king, which constitutes the spiritual, and legal, head of the family. During the era of the Apostle Paul's culture, women were asked to follow certain cultural traditions to honor the Gospel and to remain effective in their Christian testimony to non-Christians.

Biblical Values

Values are considered the basic assumptions, beliefs, or attitudes on which principles are built; Christian families tend to be led by biblical principles. Biblical values are those taught or modeled in the Bible. Although a number of values can be identified, generally a few CORE values, which are higher in priority, are easier to identify.

The biblical values that underlie a covenant marriage begin with faith in God and a pledge of love and faithfulness to the other partner. A covenant is more than a commitment, because a commitment leaves the instigator in control, whereas a covenant implies complete surrender. Important values to Christian marriages include trust, prayer, the authority of the Bible, maturity, discipline, honesty, humility, kindness, selflessness, generosity, openness, partnership, peace, family, hospitality, interdependence, and truth. Involvement and the role of the local church are often regarded as a core value to Christian couples.

Summary

A covenant is "an agreement between two parties based on promise"; *Christian Marriage Covenant* by David Martz states "covenant was in the heart of God from the day he created mankind…it carries with it the guarantee of all the benefits and blessings of that relationship." Covenants governed relationships in biblical times. Many Christian scholars believe that marriage should be understood through the concept of covenant.

The future of the institution of marriage will shape the future of society. Covenant marriages, which are based on a solemn pledge to each partner (the man and the woman) and to God, promise to strengthen marriages by making each partner accountable to God and by inviting God to be a partner in the marriage. Marriage is a private matter, yet it is also a social event that elicits a commitment from the community. The beauty of the marriage covenant is also found in biblical imagery and prophecy. The image of God in the Godhead is revealed through the loving, submissive, interdependent relationship of the marriage covenant. Another great image of covenant marriage is portrayed by the Apostle John in the marriage of the Lamb to his church (Rev. 19:7–16). The Lamb is identified as Jesus Christ and the bride is portrayed as those who have turned from their sin and believed on Jesus Christ. Covenant marriage, which was initiated, sanctioned, and protected by God, was the first social institution intended to model human relationships.

3

Love Unconditionally

The most abused and misused word in Christian circles is "love." We see from the beginning of time, that this word was used to form the world when it was in darkness. The Bible teaches in Genesis 1:1–2, that the earth was without form, and void; and darkness was on the face of the deep. And the spirit of God was hovering over the face of the water. Then God said, "Let there be light" and there was light. In fact "God" and "love" are used interchangeably. 1 John 4:8 said, he who does not love does not know God, for God is love. The very nature of God is love.

John 3:16 said for God so loved the world that he gave his only begotten son, for whosoever believeth in him should not perish, but have eternal life. The love of God transcends barriers, race, and status in life, sin, and condemnation. The Greek word for love is "agape," meaning unconditional love. A love for humanity that has no bounds, from God's perspective. In spite of human hostility, God continues to extend his love. Unconditional love is a love that is complete or guaranteed, with no conditions, limitations, or provision attached.

Paul urges the husbands and wives of the church of Ephesus to love their spouses the way God loved the church, yet in our society today, there are more Christians divorcing than non-Christians, according to statistics. It's pathetic, because Christians are the light of the world and the salt of the earth. God placed his people on this planet to shine as light. To live with the consciousness of God's existence and his love is universal.

Unconditional love should be understood as God expressing his divine love to all mankind, and not mankind expressing their love to God. For only God has the potential to express this unconditional love to humanity because of his nature and his character. God does not change. He is the same today, yesterday, and will forever be the same. He is sovereign and supreme. He never changes because of space and time. His promises are "yea and amen", they are sure. He covenants with us to keep our secrets at all times. He is divine. He changes not. Man changes in every respect of the word (change).

Man has limited potential to express this agape love, because of his sinful nature and his unpredictable character. Man's love is changeable and is contingent upon his emotions. God's love is unchangeable. Man's promises are vague and uncertain because of their human nature and sometimes character changes up. God gave Adam and Eve an opportunity to express their love, first to him and then to each other. They failed on both trials. Adam blamed his wife, Eve for giving him the fruit to eat; and she blamed the serpent for deceiving her into eating the fruit. Tragically, this blame-shame syndrome has populated the world today, especially between husbands and wives in Christian circles.

The Myth of Unconditional Love

Humanly speaking, unconditional love is a myth. That is because humans are naturally self-biased and the human heart is so deceitful that one can fool himself into thinking that he loves unconditionally, when in fact he has all kinds of conditions. For instance, what kind of "unconditional" love is at work when the psychiatrist's client can no longer pay for services and therapy is discontinued? Or when a tenant cannot reach her month's rent for one month and the landlord evicts her?

Unconditional love cannot be based upon performance or it wouldn't be unconditional. Therefore, it must be based on the intrinsic worth of the person. Paul Brownback, in his book *The Danger of Self-Love*, explains it this way:

> "...By unconditional love we are speaking of love on the basis of being rather than doing. One implication of this teaching is the place of grandeur that it gives to the human being. I am lovable just because I am human; therefore being human, in and of itself, regardless of what I do with my humanness, must have some sort of independent value or worth. It is by itself a sufficient claim to respect and esteem."

Thus, according to the self theories, everyone is born with the *right* to receive unconditional love and unconditional acceptance throughout his entire life, no matter what!

James Dobson, one of the chief proponents of unconditional love, believes that all people need it. In his article "Newlywed Nonsense", Dobson declares: Then as an extra bonus, Dobson brings God in as the primary person who gives this unconditional love and acceptance—he says, "God's acceptance is *unconditional*." Dobson is not alone in that conclusion. A host of well-respected professing Christian leaders describe God's love as unconditional.

Pastors should have been alerted to the subtleties of deception that would turn a believer's eyes from God to self. But alas, rather than warning the sheep, many of the "shepherds" have joined the psychologists and embraced their teachings of unconditional love and acceptance.

There are four Greek words that ancient Greeks used to refer to the different aspects of love.

1) Agape—means "I love you." The word "agape" translates into the verb "I love." The verb appears in the New Testament describing the relationship between Jesus and his beloved disciple, amongst other things. This agape love was expressed to describe God's love for humanity. It is clear and concise that some husbands and wives lack in this type of love in their relationships as married couples. The evidence

is clear in the gross number of divorces that occur on a daily basis. It is clear in the growing rate of single parents, the rate of homicide, etc.

The agape love is definitively associated with God above and not man. God is immutable (not subject to change) and man is mutable (capable of changing in nature, emotions, form, and quality).

2) Eros—is passionate love with sensual desire and longing. It means romantic love. Plato, a great philosopher, once said, "Eros helps the soul recall knowledge of beauty, and contribute to an understanding of spiritual truths." Lovers and philosophers are all inspired to seek truths by eros.

Eros love is matrimonial. It is meant to be shared between husbands and wives in a practical or pragmatic way. There should be no resistance between spouses.

3) Philia—means friendship in modern Greek, a dispassionate, virtuous love. It includes loyalty to friends, family, and community, and requires virtues, equality, and familiarity. In ancient texts, "philia" denoted a general type of love, used for love between family, friends, a desire or an enjoyment of an activity, as well as between lovers.

Philia love is the initial love between a man and a woman that develops over a period of time into intimacy, which subsequently leads into a marital relationship. Philia love was established with the understanding to love mankind, relatives, church, and to be hospitable. Philia love needs to have boundaries and some degree of camaraderie.

4) Storge—means affection in modern Greek; it is natural affection, like that felt by parents for their offspring. Storge love, at times, is felt between husbands' and wives' preferences and tastes for other people. Occasionally, husbands and wives find themselves approaching the opposite sex and expressing their regrets for not knowing them before they met their spouse. Storge can be bold and aggressive at times.

Those four Greek words translate into one word—love. Generally speaking, love requires work. The same amount of energy a mother may utilize taking care of her child is necessary to keep your love life going strong. It is not a piece of cake. God exerts lots of patience and tolerance with us on a daily basis; he knows how to go the extra mile even when we are at fault. He overlooks our weaknesses and realizes we are vulnerable, and graciously pardons us.

He is expecting the same from us when it comes to our spouses, to be patient and kind, to look beyond their faults and weaknesses, and to pardon them, to OBEY them even when it may be the hardest thing for us to do.

You can't express your love towards your spouse unless you are willing to exercise patience and be sensitive to every movement your spouse makes. Again, picture a mother dealing with her baby, so innocent and immature, and longing for guidance. Not implying that your spouse is in any way immature, but getting to know your spouse can take years because seeing me prior to marriage and living with me are two completely different scenarios.

I have been married to my spouse for twenty-seven years, and to this day, I am still learning new things about her, and she is still learning new things about me. To develop an unbroken relationship with your spouse, you have got to be patient and kind even in the most crucial situations between both of you. Love must be nourished to grow strong and unselfish. Babies generally are being nourished by their mothers' breast milk and other food that gives them nutrients that will enable their bodies to develop stronger. In addition, mothers offer tender loving and caring at all times to their babies. Their objective is somewhat singular in purpose, which is to provide total nourishment towards the foundation of that infant's life. Likewise, both husbands and wives need to understand that love necessitates nourishment.

True love requires attention and affection. In our busy-paced world, husband and wife hardly find time to develop relationships that begin on the foundation of love, merely because of the demands that society has on their lifestyle. Everyone wants to achieve the American dream. Even if it means that he or she has to risk his or her marriage to achieve it, that's cool.

Well, frankly speaking, nothing is wrong with pursuing the American dream, but everything is wrong in risking your marriage or trading your marriage to achieve the American dream. Getting involved in relationships demands each other's attention. The big picture should reflect God's love, attention, and his affection that was demonstrated on the cross of Calvary to save us from the penalty of death. His intention was for us to translate his demonstrative attitude into our relationships, with the hope that it will be effective in generations to come.

Attention and affection alert every husband and wife to the simple fact that they need to spend quality time with their spouses. You cannot give your spouse attention and affection unless you are connected physically. Email, phone calls, and correspondence cannot take the place of that tangible experience between husband and wife. It's like removing the wire that connects the switch; there is no way that light will function in the absence of the switch. Spouses find themselves in similar situations. Whenever that link is missing, everything closes down, even if the connection was right from the beginning.

Working two jobs, and overtime, does not warrant risking the harmony of your relationship. Whenever there is a lack of fulfillment in a relationship, either party will seek ways to fill that void, especially in the areas of attention and affection. God did not create these emotions, *attention* and *affection*, only for wives, but they were meant for husbands also. Whenever there is a long absence of attention and affection, the spirit of vulnerability kicks in, thus making your spouse open to attack and damage. The husband has a responsibility to protect and serve his wife. The wife has a responsibility to complement her husband's visions and directions, and to walk in love. Attention and affection are possible when spouses begin to honor God. If you know how to honor God, then honoring your spouse will come as expected; no effort will be needed.

A Misunderstanding of God's Love

The basis for their eager embrace is a misunderstanding of "the love of Christ which passeth knowledge" (Eph. 3:19). They equate unconditional love and acceptance with the fact that God's love is vast, unfathomable, and unmerited. Then they follow that with the idea that if God loves and accepts people unconditionally, they should also love and accept themselves unconditionally. While this may sound like a logical progression, there are some serious problems with the basic assumptions.

Therefore, we must address the question: Is God's love unconditional? Or are there any conditions that must be met to become a recipient of his love?

Paul prayed that the believers in Ephesus would be able to comprehend the length, width, depth, and height of God's love. He desired that they know the love of Christ, which surpasses knowledge, so that they would be filled with the fullness of God (Eph. 3:16–19). The wide expanse of God's love has been the theme of the Gospel throughout the ages, for to know his love is to know him. Therefore, any consideration of his love is highly important and must be based upon his revelation of himself, rather than upon the imagination of men.

Love According to Secular Humanism

Ever since the rise of secular humanism in this country, and especially since the establishment of humanistic psychology, the popular, "relevant" term to describe God's love has been "unconditional." The thrust of this word in humanistic psychology has been both to give and to expect unconditional love from one another with *no strings attached*. While unconditional love and acceptance supposedly promote change and growth, they make no requirements. But God, who is love, requires change and enables his children to grow in righteousness.

In humanistic psychology, parents and society are always the culprits. Since they believe that every person is born with intrinsic worth and innate goodness, psychologists contend that one main reason people experience emotional and behavioral problems is because they have not received unconditional love from their parents. Following that thesis, Christians have come to believe that the best kind of love is unconditional love. It is the highest love secular humanists know. It is thought of as a love that *makes no demands for performance, good behavior, or the like*. It has also been associated with a kind of permissiveness, since it makes no demands and has no conditions, even though the promoters of the unconditional love jargon would say that unconditional love does not have to dispense with discipline.

God's Love Revealed through Scripture

Because the concept of unconditional love permeates society and because it is often thought of as the highest form of human love, it is natural for a Christian to mistakenly use this term to describe God. After all, his love is far greater than any human love imaginable. God's love for humanity is so great that "He gave his only begotten Son that whosoever believeth in him should not perish, but have everlasting life" (John 3:16). Oh, the magnitude of the cost! We cannot even fathom his love even though our very breath depends upon it! His love indeed reaches to the heights and depths. But again, is God's love truly unconditional?

God's love is available to human beings by grace alone. There is nothing that men can do to earn that love. There is no good work that is either demanded or even possible. But does that make God's love unconditional? "That whosoever will" is most certainly not a work, but it *is* a condition. Otherwise we would end up with universalism (all people saved) rather than salvation by grace received *through* faith.

God chooses upon whom he will place his love and the benefits of his love. Did Jesus ever imply that God's love is unconditional? He said to his disciples:

> "He that hath my commandments, *and keepeth them,* he
> it is that loveth me; and he that loveth me shall be loved
> of my Father, and I will love him, and will manifest
> myself to him" (John 14:21).

One might argue that the story of the prodigal son (Luke 15:11) proves unconditional love (as Charles Stanley teaches). It indeed illustrates the vastness of God's love, forgiveness, and long-suffering. However, the son repented*!* If he had a prosperous evil life, he might never have repented. And while the father would have waited and hoped, he would not have extended his love. After all, he did not go out searching for him to support his folly.

Up to a point, this seems to indicate unconditional love, and yet, God is not waiting in ignorance, not knowing what those for whom his Son died might be doing. It is difficult enough to understand God's love without adding the term "unconditional love," which is loaded with secular, humanistic, psychological connotations. The story of the prodigal son teaches grace, forgiveness, and mercy—but unconditional love? No!

While God loves with a greater love than humans can comprehend, his holiness and justice also must be taken into consideration. Therefore, the term "unconditional love" is inadequate for defining God. It does not account for God's reaction to pompous men who devise plans against him and his anointed. The psalmist goes so far as to say:

> "He that sitteth in the heavens shall laugh: the Lord shall
> have them in derision. Then shall he speak to them in his
> wrath, and vex them in his sore displeasure" (Ps. 2:4–5).

And what about Lot's wife as she turned to look at the smoldering cities? Or what about Jesus' words to the cities that refused to repent? Does this sound like unconditional love?

> "Woe to thee, Chorazin! Woe unto thee, Bethsaida!
> For if the mighty works, which were done in you, had
> been done in Tyre and Sidon, they would have repented
> long ago in sackcloth and ashes. But I say unto you, it
> shall be more tolerable for Tyre and Sidon at the Day of
> Judgment, than for you. And thou, Capernaum, which
> art exalted unto heaven, shalt be brought down to hell…
> it shall be more tolerable for the land of Sodom in the
> Day of Judgment, than for thee" (Matt. 11:21–24).

Conclusion

But perhaps one could say that God's love for the Christian is unconditional, since the Christian partakes of his love and grace through faith. Wouldn't it be better to say that the conditions have been met? Jesus met the first condition, to wash away the sin that God hates. The believer meets the second condition, but only by God's grace through faith.

Or perhaps it would be better to say that *God's love extended to a person is conditioned by his plan to give eternal life to those whom he has enabled to believe on his Son. The conditions of God's love are resident within himself.* As our opening Bible verse says: "He hath made us accepted!"

There is a strong temptation to use vocabulary that is popular in society to make Christianity sound relevant. Christians have something far better than what the world offers, but in expressing that good news, they confuse people by using words that are already loaded with humanistic connotations and systems of thought. It would be better not to use the expression "unconditional love" when describing God's love. There are plenty of other good words (1 John 4:9–10, 16):

> In this was manifested the love of God towards us, because that God sent his only begotten Son into the world, that we might live through him.

> Herein is love, not that we love God, but that he loved us, and sent his Son to be the propitiation for our sins.

And we have known and believe the love that God hath to us. 1 John 4:16–"God is love; and he that dwelled in love dwelled in God and God in him." The incomprehensible magnitude of God's love surpasses any concept of love devised by humanistic psychologists. The doctrine of unconditional love is considered to be a myth that glorifies man rather than God.

4

The Power of Agreement in Marriage

One of the most productive disciplines in any union is agreement. For where there is a spark of agreement, the relationship of a wife and husband will grow. Agreement is the spirit that complements each other. Years ago, there was no need for an agreement in a union, since the man or the husband terrorized his wife. He felt because he worked and brought the money home, he had the right to call the shots in his home. Well, over the years that has been changed. It's a new day, a new season, new society with new order.

Most women are independent rather than dependent upon their husband for finances and other necessities that are financially related. Not only that they are independent, but in addition they are making great strides in the professional world, in terms of their job description and the office they occupy. Responsibilities have shifted somewhat from the man to the woman. This paradigm has caused tremendous difficulties in relationships that were doing great for a period of time, but now those same relationships are going through all kinds of changes.

Many husbands are literally confused about this dilemma, which has taken our society by storm.

Needless to say, there are couples that were spending thousands of dollars to see the most prominent counselors and psychologists in town for solutions to this crippling dilemma, but their searches were in vain. Subsequently, they tried the court to solve their problems, but instead of their problems being solved, they became worse and ultimately, divorce parted their friendship. To avoid long lines and wasted hours in courthouses and around the desk of a psychiatrist, husbands and wives need to follow the Golden Rule. It is said that prevention is better than cure…The Golden Rule is built upon the word of God. He is the initiator and author of marriage; he must know what is good for us.

When it comes to marriage, the first golden rule is that husbands and wives have a responsibility to love each other with the love of God or the God kind of love. Some spouses' love runs out whenever they see someone who they think is better than their spouse, such as in looks, education, positions, or even their success. Husbands and wives need to love each other through thick or thin, in the good times or in the bad times do the same. No one and nothing should come between your relationships.

As a matter of fact, if there is true love or the God kind of love, nothing should be able to penetrate the relationship. The Bible says that a man should leave his father and mother, and "cleave" means to hold on to each other like a leech or a pest. 1 Corinthians 13:5 says love does not seek its own, is not provoked, thinks no evil. Love is steady, and God is love.

The second golden rule in marriage, when it comes to agreement, comes from Amos 3:3. Can two walk together except they agree? The breeding ground for agreement is love. John 3:16 says God so loved the world that he gave his only begotten Son to die in the world's stead. Jesus had to first be in agreement with his father before he voluntarily gave his life for the world. His obedience demonstrates not only his love, but also some degree of agreement. Agreement is when someone admits, concedes, to get along together. God the Father, God the Son, and God the Holy Spirit are always in agreement and will always be. Amos 3:3 points out that unless two walk together, there will be no agreement.

Agreement is an act of union or an act of permission granted to tolerate or put up with one another.

It is virtually impossible for husbands and wives to walk together (continue in union) if there is no agreement between them. In cases of disagreement, the question will always be who was wrong, is it the husband or the wife? I think we need to back up and rephrase that question. Instead of asking who was wrong, we need to evaluate their level of maturity. It doesn't matter who was wrong, but rather who is more mature. The mature person should always take the lower seat, even if he or she has done right. The more one matures, the more he or she becomes humble, and less arrogant. When you walk together, it calls for patience, wisdom, knowledge, understanding, and forgiveness.

For more than eighteen years, my wife and I have been walking together in the God kind of love, a love that is unselfish and unparalleled with the world's kind of love. Our accomplishment of this bonding was not because we have not experienced differences of opinion and gone through changes like any other couple, but rather because we have made up our minds to love each other in spite of every barrier that might want to interfere with our relationship. We have taken an oath before God and man to stick it out, come hell or high water. Whenever there is an issue between us, we choose to talk about it, pray over it, and talk about it until we resolve it. In my own experiences, I have grown to realize that communication plays a major role in marriage. As a matter of fact, communication builds a bridge over troubled water. It mobilizes the couple to meet at a common ground of reasoning and reconciliation. Husbands and wives need to spend more time in praying together and communicating, and less time arguing with each other. This approach will definitely alleviate fights in your marriage.

The third golden rule in marriage, when it comes to agreement, comes from Matthew 18: 19–20: I say unto you, that if two of you shall agree on earth as touching anything that they shall agree ask, it shall be done for them of my father which is in heaven; for where two or three are gathered together in my name, there I am in the midst of them. The key word in Matthew 18:19 is "touching." Before we touch, we need to establish a level of agreement mentally and physically. There are many physical agreements but no mental agreement; therefore, no power emerges from that kind of agreement. It cannot be half done, but must be complete all the way. God's word says, "if two shall agree," not one. You are no more twain but one. This means that if the husband is thinking to purchase a home for the good of the family, the wife should not be thinking to purchase the latest model of Nissan Altima automobile. Rather, she should bring her thoughts under subjection to her husband's thoughts to purchase a home. God says if this is possible, then the home will be possible.

Husbands and wives are constantly engaged in a tug-of-war where their future is concerned, resulting in poor choices of material gains and a relationship that will ultimately end up in divorce if they are being neglectful.

God's initial and future intention for mankind is that of agreement. It is quite evident that the first man and first woman who God created (Adam and Eve) had failed recklessly because of poor agreement skills. They failed in the act of obeying the devil and disobeying the voice of God. They failed in the act of agreeing who is in authority, if it was the devil or God. They even failed in the act of disagreement, to say, "sorry," for their sins toward God. In contrast, God entered into an agreement or a contract with his Son, Jesus, the second person of the Godhead, and the Holy Spirit, the third person of the Godhead, to deliver mankind from their sins.

Husbands and wives will have to make sacrifices in some cases to reach the place of agreement. Sometimes to get to a common agreement, it will involve time, money, courage, wisdom, and the Holy Spirit. The writer would like to recommend twelve essentials that would prevent disagreement between husbands and wives.

1. Don't be selfish with your opinion.
2. Give your partner the benefit of the doubt.
3. Admit when you are wrong.
4. Learn to say, "I am sorry"
5. Don't blame your spouse when it is your fault.
6. Learn the art of forgiveness.

7. Be fair, be frank.
8. Pray together as often as possible.
9. Don't take each other for granted.
10. Be sensitive when your spouse is in pain.
11. Communicate to conquer issues in the relationship.
12. Don't discuss your intimate problems with others.

Being in agreement should not be contingent upon what Hollywood portrayed or what society defined as agreement, but rather what God's word is saying; husbands and wives should live their lives based upon the principles of God's words. They should be constantly seeking God's guidance and help. Being in agreement is not a cheap commodity for husbands and wives to be in control of. Remember, if God said it is possible, believe it, accept it, and declare it. It is all yours.

5

The Power of Prayer in Marriage

Getting your spouse to pray is not a magical formula, but rather a sign of unity and covenant. Because of the way America has designed life for the family, prayer for many has become a burden, especially for working spouses. Prayer in our marital experience should become a priority; both parties, husband and wife, need to have a strong desire for prayer since both of them would be the beneficiary of the manifestation of God's presence.

In my family, my wife and I have developed and established a strategy to be consistent in prayer. Each morning when we rise, we pray one for another. There are times when my wife gets a little tired and does not feel like getting up. That's the time when I take the initiative and intercede for her, realizing that my office in my home is of the prophet, priest, and king. All three of these offices have great significance when it comes to supreme rulership over the people and also a God-given responsibility to intercede on the people's behalf.

Many of our homes are weak because men have lost their office in the homes. They have become self-centered and self-sufficient...hence the reason why there is no place for God. God has called man to be not only the keeper of the family, but also the protector and provider of both physical and spiritual guidance. He has given man authority and leadership skills so as to demonstrate dominion on earth. But sad to say, man has chosen another path that displeases God and his order in the kingdom.

1 Peter 3 admonishes the family to cultivate godly living in the home. It reminds the wives to be submissive to their own husbands, even if they are not godly men. The writer is aware of the fact that it is hard for godly women to accept, especially if their husbands are not trying to be better. I have known several men who have beautiful Christian wives, who love the Lord with all of their hearts, but the husbands are alcoholics, drug addicts, perverts, gays, and some even associate themselves with being "down-low" (married men who have intimate relationships with other men, unknown to their wives). God is saying in the gospel of 1 Peter 3, amidst their crucial condition, as wives you have a responsibility to obey them because of the covenant (promise) vows you took in marriage.

Infidelity is one of the reasons why barriers are created between husbands and wives; subsequently those barriers turn into a battleground. This is where the devil gets the victory, thus sowing discord. The one word that is lacking is "obedience." Not only the wife has a responsibility to obey God's word, but also the husband, according to 1 Peter 3:7; Peter calls upon the husbands to dwell with their wives with understanding, since they are the weaker vessel. Also, since they are heirs together of the grace of God, that their prayers may not be hindered. I perceived that prayers are being hindered every minute in our society, especially when we think about the constant stream of prayer requests every day, most being for marital relationships that are on the verge of breaking up.

I alluded in previous paragraphs that God made men to be leaders in their homes. Unless men return to their rightful place in the home, the home will never be what God ordained it to be. In Joshua 24, Joshua was not looking at what was happening in his neighbor's home. He established a one-track mind because of the way the children of Israel were behaving. He declared, "as for me and my house, we will serve the Lord." We need more Joshua type men in our society today. History has proven that a foundation of a strong nation begins with the home. If the homes were strong, we would have strong churches, schools, communities, and subsequently the entire nation would be strong. More prayer more power, less prayer less power. The devil always tries to rob us of our full potential when it comes to entering to the very presence of God.

After I got married, my wife and I established family devotions in our home. We gather every Friday night to celebrate the Sabbath of the Lord our God together in fellowship. This is an act of acknowledgment and thanksgiving for all the things that God has done for us. It is also a good way of cultivating good morale and building character in our children's lives. Tragically, however, whenever we kneeled to pray, the enemy would subtly put our children to sleep. Subsequently, we extended our family devotion to once per week in the morning, where we experienced the same problem of spiritual drowsiness that penetrated the minds of our children. Nevertheless, as parents, our determination and desire is to be a model to our children when it comes to prayers. Prayer should be paramount in every marital relationship. Prayer moves the hands and mind of God. It takes you into a different realm of relationship with God. It also takes you to places that you have never been before.

The only solution and antidote for the rising rate of divorce and broken covenants is prayer. Prayer cements and stabilizes relationships. Prayer heals wounds and renews strength. William McGill said, "The value of consistent prayer is not that he will hear us, but that we will hear him." He also states "Prayer may not change things for you, but it sure changes you for things." For my twenty-seven years of marriage, I am not ashamed to declare that prayer plays the most important part in my wife's and I relationship. It's an honor to declare that it was through prayers I experienced the manifestation of my vision for my wife. Currently, prayers are the key to our success in marriage.

Amos 3:3 declares that two cannot walk together unless they agree. The power of agreement is prayer. Disagreement between husbands and wives is inevitable, in spite of their background in education, their financial possessions, creed, and culture. Verbal conflict will surface even if it's on the basis of sex and romance or in-law problems. Can you imagine that a wife would divorce her husband because he snores too hard at night? It seems to me that she married him for his holy quietness and not for his emotion. God has called us to the knee city. If we get down on our knees at the midnight hours and seek his face for his presence, power, and love, he will honor our prayers. There are various artists that sing the song "Down on my Knees" which declares that they found whatever answers they were searching for down on their knees.

Husbands and wives should see the need to pray on a regular basis. The Bible admonishes us to pray without ceasing. Prayer is when you talk to God and God talks to you. It's a dialogue, not a monologue. Meditation is when you listen to God. Oswald Chambers said, "We have to pray with our eyes on God not on the difficulties," and "When a man is at his wits end it is not a cowardly thing to pray, it is the only way he can get in touch with reality." Prayers should mold them, shape them, fashion their ways, strengthen their thoughts, and decrease their sins.

Based upon the word of God, prayer involves several important essentials, such as:

Faith:

The most meaningful prayer between husband and wife comes from the heart that places its trust in the Lord, in spite of difficulties in the relationship. Each spouse has a responsibility to appropriate his or her faith in Jesus Christ whenever a crisis hits the very office that God has honored. Complaining, murmuring, then quitting is definitely the fastest way out of a marital covenant. Especially whenever the going gets tough. But one little act of turning around and bowing before the God who said, "What God joined together let no man put asunder," could definitely make the wounded whole again.

I was privileged to counsel Christian couples that had serious crises in their marital relationships, such as poor communication skills, jealousy, selfishness, greed, and a long list of other things that literally poisoned, corrupted, and ruined their relationships. I have found out that the common reason for crisis in their relationship was because of a poor prayer life. The second reason was a lack of communication. Well, if you are not communicating with God on a regular basis, it would be difficult for you to communicate with your spouse on a regular basis. Faith is the driving force behind your lack. Faith will motivate you to rise up and pray up. The Bible says, but without faith it is impossible to please him; for he that cometh to God must first believe that he is God, and that he is a rewarder of those who diligently seek him." (Hebrews 11:6)

God speaks to us through the Bible, and we speak to one another in trustful, believing terms. Assured by the scriptures that God is personal, living, active, all knowing, all wise and all-powerful, we know by faith that God can help us. A confident prayer life is built on the cornerstone of faith in Jesus Christ. God hears prayer when we literally feel the hurt for our spouse during our intercession with God. God declares in his word that he has been touched with the feelings with our infirmities and with his stripes we are healed. Spiritually speaking, we ought to be touched with our spouse's feelings. If we are touched when we intercede on their behalf, then deliverance is inevitable.

Worship:

During worship we (husbands and wives) should be able to recognize what is of highest worth. Of course, that won't be ourselves, others, our work, but God. Only the highest divine being deserves our highest respect. Guided by scriptures, husbands and wives should set their values in accordance with God's will and perfect standards, before God's angel, and hide their faces and cry, "Holy, holy is the Lord of hosts." Worship needs to be a way of life or a lifestyle that would provoke the presence of God to enter into the mind of mankind. True worship between spouses will subsequently give permission for a demonstration of longevity in their relationship.

Praise:

Every couple needs to be in the attitude of praise, since the natural outgrowth of faith, worship, confession, and adoration is praise. Praise gives freedom to their differences of opinion. It stimulates the thoughts towards oneness. Praise captures and arrests the very presence of God, especially during devotions. Praise has the ability to move the relationship to the next level. Every couple needs to make praise to God their daily priority. They need to praise him individually and collectively, depending upon the occasion. The Bible says that God inhabits our praises. He dwells in our praises. Praises attract the very presence of God. The psalmist David exclaimed in Psalm 150:6, Let everything that has breath praise the Lord, praise ye the Lord.

Forgiveness:

Asking God to forgive sins, hurting one another, for acting selfish with a spouse, and a long list of other issues is not a choice for couples that are serious about relationship, but rather the only option. Pleading to the only one who can forgive us for our trespasses is paramount for our prayers being answered positively. Unforgivable sin creates a barrier between God and man and between husbands and wives. Being unforgiving has the ability to stagnate you from reaching your full potential in prayer for yourself, your spouse, or other persons and things of interest.

Forgiveness is the act of excusing or pardoning your spouse, in spite of his or her slight shortcomings, and errors (allowing room for error or weaknesses). I believe that Jesus wants us to come clean, he wants us to remove our masks and humble ourselves before him. In Isaiah 55:1, he calls us unto reasoning in spite of our weakness and sins. Breakthrough and victory in our prayers manifest only when we seek God through forgiveness.

6

Communication is Imperative in Marriage

The word "communication" comes from the Latin verb "communicate," to talk together, confer, and consult one with another. It is intimately related to the Latin word "communions," which means not only community but also fellowship and justice in one's dealings with another. Communication is a transaction process rather than an interaction process. In the transactional process, all persons are engaged in sending (encoding) and receiving (decoding) messages simultaneously. Husband and wife are constantly sharing in the encoding and the decoding process, and each person is affecting the other.

This way, your marriage won't dry up and become routine. Communication is critical for a healthy marriage. Some people describe the ideal marriage as a two-way street. If you don't have any arguments, or one side is always directing the traffic, you are riding on a one-way street without any communication. That's not something to cheer about since communication has to do with decoding (receiving) and encoding (sending) for communication to take place.

Establish a Healthy Communication Technique

Maybe people have different views about the true meaning of the word "argument." The husband and wife are two distinct bodies. Arguments are just part of life. What is important is how you handle those arguments. You'll need to communicate with some skill. Men and women are different, so oftentimes they "talk" but fail to "communicate." This only makes matters worse. Couples need to find an effective method of communication. Communication is often the major player in holding a marriage together. Unfortunately, many couples lack this skill and desperately need to work on it.

Couples must learn to understand each other better and recognize and accept each other's point of view. When you love but don't fully appreciate each other, you'll be destined to have a rocky journey ahead. When couples are willing to talk about everything and step into each other's shoes to look at problems, then that will be the starting point of an ideal marriage. Galatians 5:22 tells us that the fruit of the spirit is love (the chief of the fruit), the main ingredient in a healthy relationship. When there is love, communication is and will always be possible. Many couples do not communicate well because they can't tolerate each other. Love transcends behavior, emotions, and culture barriers. Love empties itself for fellowship, because fellowship breeds unity and unity is strength. The more husbands and wives communicate, the closer their relationship will grow. Growth comes through nurturing and caring for each other. The quantity of a farmer's crop is determined by how much time he puts into the garden. Likewise, communication is a measuring rod that determines how much you care for each other.

Communication is an Art

Experts believe communication can be divided into five levels:

1. Level of Acquaintance
2. Sharing of Information
3. Sharing of Ideas

4. Sharing of Emotions
5. Gut-Level Sharing

Wives often want a husband who can sit down and listen, someone who can completely appreciate their emotions and views. Husbands very seldom want to reason, but when they do, they sometimes give a lecture. In this kind of situation, the wives may sometimes feel that they are talking to a wall. Eventually, the wives may stop sharing many of their feelings and thoughts. Thus, it becomes necessary for couples to learn how to communicate effectively.

In addition, couples need to love and accept each other, learn to listen, and listen with undivided attention. Be proactive, objective, and pay attention for any signs your lover may give. Learn how to talk and praise your lover frequently. Don't forget to use some humor at times. And most importantly, say everything to your lover with the love that comes straight from your heart.

The Art of Marital Communication

Marital communication is an art. It can be nurtured into the joy that God intended for couples. Try the following steps to make it happen.

- As a couple before God, commit yourselves to the recovery of a Trinitarian communication. Ask him to nurture the language of intimacy and relationship in your lives. Great communication begins with God's ears that hear and eyes that see—the Lord has made them both (Prov. 20:12).

- Accept the fact that God alone is the perfect communicator. Your marriage will always need his redeeming touch for intimate communication to develop. And you will never arrive at the place of perfect communication in marriage. For the eyes of the Lord are on the righteous and his ears are attentive to their prayer, but the face of the Lord is against those who do evil (Ps. 34:15).

- Recognize that there will be times of spontaneous communication as well as structured communication in your marriage. So be sensitive to both. Grab it when the need bursts into your marriage. Plan it when you are strung out on life's pressures. A person finds joy in giving an apt answer—how good is a timely word (Prov. 15:23). The right word at the right time is like a custom-made piece of jewelry (Prov. 25:11).

- Beware of the power of your words, both for healing and for hurting. The goal of good marital communication is "light rather than heat." The tongue has the power of life and death, and those who love it will eat its fruit (Prov. 18:21). An anxious heart weights a person down, but a kind word cheers him up (Prov. 12:25); the tongue that brings healing is a tree of life, but a deceitful tongue crushes the spirit (Prov. 12:25, 15:4). Pleasant words are like honeycomb, sweet to the soul and healing to the bones (Prov. 16:24). When words are many, sin is not absent, but the one who holds his tongue is wise (Prov. 10:19). Reckless words pierce like a sword, but the tongue of the wise brings healing (Prov. 12:18).

- Focus on listening to your mate—really listening—before speaking. Listen with two sets of ears: to the obvious words of the mouth and the not so obvious words of the heart. The heart of the righteous weighs its answers, but the mouth of the wicked gushes evil (Prov. 15:28). Even a fool is thought wise if he keeps silent, and discerning if he holds his tongue (Prov. 17:28). The one who answers before listening—that is his folly and his shame (Prov. 18:13).

- Look for things for which you can praise your mate—there are more than enough for daily appreciation. Praise is the daily bread of good marital communication. Thank God for the gift of your mate. A man is praised according to his wisdom, but men with warped minds are despised (Prov. 12:8). Charm is deceptive, and beauty is fleeting; but a woman who fears the Lord is to be praised. Give her the reward she has earned, and let her works bring her praise at the city gate (Prov. 31:30–31).

7

The Magic Words in Marriage

Children are being taught to say the basic words (magic words) that would help them through life. Words like "thank you," "excuse me" and so on. That is scarce in our world today. When I was growing up, magic words were very commonplace because we were cultured and trained to use magic words before our parents gave us their attention in any matter.

Strange enough, it's no different with married couples. After the wedding vows, couples have a tendency to forget the importance of verbalizing the magic words in their marriage. For this reason, the relationship loses the real meaning of union. I would like to share ten magic phrases that every couple needs to know and practice on a regular basis in their marital relationship.

1. "I love you"

Even though the word "love" is the most misused and abused word in the English vocabulary, when it's coming from your spouse your heart will catch on fire. Whenever the statement "I love you" is left unspoken in a relationship, it causes lots of trouble. People need to have a sense of belonging or being part of a relationship. When spouses begin to feel lonely in their relationship, the magic words, "I love you," need to be spoken into their spirit. 1 Corinthians 13:13 says that love is the greatest of faith, hope, and love. Love sends chills down the spine. Love rejuvenates happiness and peace in the relationship. Love restores and reminds couples of the good old past. The magic word "love" quickens spouses' unbelief to belief. I try to call my wife every day at work to tell her that I love her. Whenever two o'clock passes and she does not hear from me, she will call me to find out what's up. The magic words, "I love you," cement our relationship and gives it meaning.

2. "Maybe you are right"

These magic words assure couples that there is nothing like a perfect relationship, in spite of one's opinion and teaching. A minister friend of mine was telling me a true story about this pastor who allowed his wife to control the church in and out of his presence, resulting in a great falling away. She would stand up openly and rebuke the elders, deacons, and members of the congregation. One day she realized that the church was falling apart; she stood up and told her husband that maybe he was right. Those magic words, in his judgment, revolutionized the congregation in growth, by leaps and bounds. It's great when Mrs. Always Right can confess periodically to Mr. Always Wrong. I fail at times to see my wife's point, since she is more detailed than I am. I'll quickly, however, confess to her that she is right.

We can eliminate argument in our relationship if we are honest. Dishonesty breeds contempt. Acknowledging your wrong is not a crime, but rather good for your soul. Honesty is the best policy. Giving away your right for peace, longevity in marriage, and prosperity is healthy. Men generally are ashamed to say to their wives, "Maybe you are right"—they feel that making such a statement will destroy their manhood, which is not truthful. The Bible says that he that humbles himself shall be exalted. And he that exalts himself shall be abased. It is also said that the humblest calf sucks the most milk.

3. "How can I show you I love you today?"

Yes, I know these words sound antiquated, completely out of context and out of tune, not familiar at all. Well, sure enough, that's what happens when romance is on the verge of dying. Especially when promises are made, but never get executed. The qualifying word within the magic word is "show." Not only say "show," but do it now, for actions speak louder than words. Stop talking, and start acting. Demonstrate what you say now. The word "show" means to illustrate, to prove or to display as evidence. Instead of saying it, do it.

Taking home a rose or buying your wife her favorite music is showing her how much you love her. Females prefer to receive favors rather than demanding them. Showing love to your spouse needs to be done on a daily basis by both spouses. Saying it but refusing to do it is a shame. We need to say it and endorse it by our act of demonstration.

4. "Let's try it your way"

One of our biggest enemies is "Me, myself, and I." Thinking about one's self is selfish and stupid. John Donne, who is a notable poet and philosopher, said "No man is an island." But everybody needs somebody. This fact is being demonstrated even in the membership of our bodies. Whenever my feet move, my whole body moves, because every part of the body is all connected to each other. They cooperate in their respective discipline and function. Relationship calls for negotiation. It doesn't always have to be my way, but let's try it your way. Cultural upbringing can be one reason that you should use the phrase "Let's try it your way." For instance, whenever my wife and I are in the kitchen and she plans to cook ackee and codfish, I always use the magic words, "Let's try it your way," knowing that it is one of her culture's dishes.

On the contrary, whenever she is trying to cook any dish that is from my culture and I am in the kitchen, she uses the magic words, "Let's try it your way." We always accept each other's views, not just saying, "It's my way or the highway." These magic words breed camaraderie. They enhance relationship, and maximize unselfishness; consequently guarantee a lasting relationship. The life lesson here is that spouses should meet each other halfway to agree on the basis of fairness.

5. "I appreciate"

The magic is in these two simple words, "I appreciate." These two magic words will make others feel close to you and create loyal relationships. Don't be like the husband who told his wife on their wedding day, "I'm telling you now that I love you, and if that ever changes, I'll let you know." To have a great relationship, you must continually let people know that you care about them and appreciate them.

APPRECIATION—THE KEY TO GREAT RELATIONSHIPS.

Obviously, you know to say, "Thank you," when someone gives you a gift or does something special for you. However, if you're seriously interested in improving your relationship with your spouse, you need to let them know how much you appreciate things that are not special. There are the things that we just take for granted because our spouses are supposed to do them anyway. Start today by saying, "I appreciate," you for all those little things. Making a simple phone call or writing a short note only takes a minute or two. Tell your wife you appreciate her pleasant smile. "It makes me look forward to coming home." To your husband say, "I appreciate your taking out the trash, and helping the kids with their homework," etc.

The Appreciation Magnet

Appreciation makes people feel valued, and accepted. These powerful attributes act like a magnet to attract people to you and make them trust you.

How You Will Benefit

Just think of all the benefits you can get simply by saying, "I appreciate you."

- You will feel happier because you are focusing on how others are making your life better, not on their shortcomings.
- You will feel more successful because, even though your life is not perfect, you will be living with an attitude of gratitude for what you have now.

- You will be creating an atmosphere of acceptance both at work and at home.
- You will receive more cooperation from coworkers, and family.
- You will receive more appreciation for yourself in return.

Get Creative

If it makes such a difference, why don't more spouses show their appreciation? It's probably because most spouses consider writing thank you notes a chore. Here's how you can stay creative and have fun.

- Cover your thank you letters with the words, "Thank You," in different sizes of lettering.
- Make your own colorful thank you cards in celebration of your spouse's birthday or anniversary
- Give decorated "Thank You" cookies for supper
- Buy thank you gifts occasionally for your spouse.
- Write a thanksgiving poem to your spouse other than on Thanksgiving Day.
- Send a quote to your spouse that is based upon thanks or appreciation.
- Along with your thank you note, include a joke
- Bake your favorite dessert and include the recipe in your gift.
- Give thank you hugs and kisses
- Give plants or flowers to express thanks.

Appreciation is like spreading man-made sunshine into the lives of your husbands and wives in some small way; it has the ability to make your life happier.

6. "Hello, I just called to say I'm thinking of you"

Most spouses are reluctant to keep check on their better half during the course of the day, or whenever they are separated from each other. The slogan, "Out of sight, out of mind," seems fitting in some spousal relationships that do not apply these magic words that can change the world for either spouse. In my twenty-seven years of marriage, I embrace this attitude of calling my wife every day at her job, just to let her know that I'm thinking about her. I know that this does something to her. Each spouse has a responsibility to provoke each other with love, to give them a sense of belonging at all times. In this stressful and fast-paced society, we need to hear some kind words during the day. At times when I called my wife, she would laugh and tell me that I made her day.

Not only do I make her day, but I believe that I also alleviate some degree of stress from her life. My wife looks forward to her call each day. If her clock strikes four and she doesn't hear from me, I'll soon hear from her. She will ask me a question like, "What happened, you don't have a wife?" and I'll ask her "What happened, you divorced me?" Both of us have our go to quote. Picking up the phone and calling your spouse sends a message of loyalty and a sense of care for her soul. Every husband knows if their wives really care, and every wife knows if their husbands really care. Action speaks louder than voice.

7. "How I am doing as a spouse and partner?"

What a question to ask your spouse, especially when you are not sure about your love tank level. The "Love Tank Level" is the level of your love towards your spouse in any given day, from one to ten, one being the lower or empty and ten being the higher or full tank. A car stops running when the gas runs out. Likewise, some spouses stop functioning when the good times are few. Some unions are built on approvals. Unless you approve what I am doing, I can't function. In my union, I am self-motivated. My wife has no reason to treat me like a robot.

I know my basic responsibility as a father and a husband, and she knows her basic responsibility as a mother and a wife. However, a tap on the shoulder every so often helps to motivate our ego. Approvals were not meant to be silent, but rather spoken. Someone said that encouragement sweetens labor. The more we encourage each other, the greater the result will be. On the contrary, the more you discourage each other, the poorer the result will be. We are responsible to approve of our spouses even when they don't deserve our approval. Showing this commitment will keep their love tank level going.

8. "I'm sorry I hurt you"

This statement is so necessary, yet at times so hard to say. Every civilized human being knows right from wrong, because we were created with a conscience. These magic words, "I'm sorry I hurt you," should be frequently used in every union. Husbands and wives should realize that they are not perfect, but rather vulnerable. Hence the reason "I'm sorry I hurt you" needs to be prevalent in our vocabulary. Husbands and wives need to practice these magic words for the following reasons:

- To prevent a miserable relationship.
- To avoid divorce.
- To prevent intruders.
- To maintain a high level of intimacy with your spouse.

Saying, "I'm sorry," is an act of confession or admitting that you have done wrong and you are willing to overcome and move on. This helps the relationship to be stable and grow stronger. It also builds trust and longevity. "I'm sorry I hurt you" is biblical terminology, because the Bible literally speaks of several individuals who express their wrongful and willful act to their opponent by taking responsibility for their own action.

9. "Please forgive me"

Every husband and wife who lived long enough together would automatically add these words into their vocabulary: "Please forgive me." We are vulnerable because of self and sin, which overpower us and cause us to do everything that is wrong when our objective is to do good. The enemy knows our weakness; he takes joy in deceiving us. The Bible teaches that he comes to kill, steal, and destroy. From creation, the enemy has been trying hard to deceive humanity. In the book of Genesis, the Bible says the devil succeeded in working through the woman Eve to get at her husband Adam. Ultimately, they sought God's forgiveness for their faults.

This was another victory for the enemy. The Bible said that if we sin we have an advocate who is willing and just to forgive us of all our sins and to cleanse us from all unrighteousness. God doesn't function like man. Man carries issues for years, but God instantaneously forgives and forgets. Pride sometimes prevents husbands and wives asking their spouses to forgive them, especially if they know that they have done something that was rude and out of place. This can lead to a bitter relationship because of the absence of the magic words, "Please forgive me," in the relationship.

Court TV is a good demonstration of how husbands and wives break their covenants to be separated from each other for reasons such as: because her husband utilizes her credit card without gratitude to his spouse, so she is seeking a divorce. Or because either party cheated, this became the basis for divorce. If love were there from the beginning of the union, then divorce should not be an option, but rather an expression of, "Please forgive me." Every human heart needs to submit to these magic words, simply because one never knows when his day of imperfection shall show up. The proverbial phrase says, "every dog has his day."

10. "Honey"

Addressing your wife as "honey" sends a message of sweetness and caring. Most wives associate this magic word, "honey," with the natural sweetness that comes from a beehive. And since "honey" defines sweetness, they submit faster to that which it implies. Mostly husbands use the magic word "honey" as a means of coaching their wives. It solicits their attention toward a favor etc. Husbands use honey to motivate or "butter up" their spouse. There are times when I want a favor done by my wife, and I know that because of the nature of the favor, my wife would pitch a fit, so I'll use a magic word like "honey," and I'll let her know that she is the best thing that has ever happened to me...not that I'm bribing her, but I use that platform as an opportunity to express myself to her, and at the same time look forward for my favor to be accomplished. Sometimes it works. Sometimes it doesn't.

Husbands and wives need to know their spouses' soft spots. They need to be familiar with the right button to push to get things done. We need to take time to learn our spouse. If you know when to add oil to your car engine, you may never experience any major problem with your engine. Sad to say, a great number of spouses are unfamiliar with their partners' tender spots, thus a negative response. To know her is to love her. Unless you know your spouse, you may not be able to love her effectively. Husbands, let your honey be realistic, let it flow from the heart.

8

The Importance of Finance in Marriage

Money is defined as any marketable goods or token used by a society as a store of value, a medium of exchange or a unit of account. Money objects can meet some or all of these needs. Since the need arises naturally, societies organically create a money object when none exists. In other cases, a central authority creates a money object; this is more frequently the case in modern society with paper money.

Like planning a wedding, deciding how to manage money is a matter of taste and consideration. Deciding with whom you will spend the rest of your life certainly affects how the cash would be handled. There are no right or wrong answers, but for couples who are compatible, getting married means "becoming one." When you choose a person to spend the rest of your life with, no one can make that decision for you. The same applies when deciding how to manage money; you and your spouse have to determine what works for the good of the marriage.

Successful financial management is be determined by the couple's personalities, their background in financial management, and their ultimate motive and objectives in marriage. What works for one couple might not necessarily work for another. Some people enter into marriage to see how much financial gain they can accumulate from the union for themselves. On the other hand, some people enter into the union with the aim to work together for one common good when it comes to their finances.

Statistics tells us that lack of finances or poor financial management in a marital relationship is the second reason for divorce. The importance of finance in marriage should not only be taught, but put into practice; managing your finances in an unpredictable society calls for more than one head and one decision maker. The Bible says, " you are no more twain but one." Gone are the days when it used to be "me, myself, and I, you are now into a covenant (a contractual binding agreement between you and your spouse).

There are six steps to champion your finances in marriage:

1. Budgeting

Budgeting is the means of handling your money wisely and professionally. Budgeting manages your income versus your spending. Budgeting helps in maintaining a healthy spending habit; it has to do with being disciplined in your spending. Before you can start your financial goals, you need to determine where you stand financially. The following is a rough draft of items and the percentage utilized for each item that the average couple budgets for, depending on the number of their household, and income scale.

1. Tithes and offering, 10 percent–14 percent
2. Monthly mortgage or rent, 20 percent–28 percent
3. Monthly insurance (car, house, life), 8 percent–10 percent
4. Groceries (food), 9 percent–12 percent
5. Utility bills, 4 percent–5 percent
6. Clothing, 3 percent–6 percent
7. Vacation, 2 percent–3 percent
8. School tuition/child care 2 percent–3 percent
9. Social activities, 1 percent–2 percent
10. Investment, 2 percent–3 percent

11. Children expenses, 1 percent–3 percent
12. Savings, 9 percent–12 percent
13. Debts, 0–6 percent
14. Medical/dental/emergency, 2 percent–4 percent
15. Other expenses/miscellaneous, 5 percent–6 percent

2. Managing Your Finances

When it comes to managing finances in a union, one person should be elected to handle the bills. In most cases, the spouse who has a stronger desire to save should be responsible for handling the bills. In my home, my wife assumes the responsibility for writing a great percentage of our bills since she has greater skills to manage money. She would literally walk two or three extra miles to save two dollars; I do not have the patience to be walking around looking for great bargains or to be tearing off coupons. The first store that meets my needs, I'll purchase in spite of cost.

The husband or wife who has been elected to manage their finances should not be the dictator, but rather have a mutual agreement or understanding. Both parties should be responsible to oversee and maintain the handling of their money. Differences are fine, but they must be recognized and compromised fairly. It should not be a "wife thing" or a "husband thing" because you were elected, but rather "our thing" because we are one.

Husbands and wives should establish a place or file to put all receipts, check stubs, withdrawal and deposit slips, and pay stubs. Put your bills in another place or file close by. At the end of each month, both parties should sit down and record all transactions made in the account and go over the bills to ensure accuracy. The checking account should be balanced whenever a check is being written, but at the end of each month it should be reviewed for accuracy and adjusted if needed.

3. Use of Financial Software

Some couples use personal finance software such as QuickBooks or Excel to organize and to keep track of their finances. These kinds of software work to the advantage of busy couples who may have a regular job and also attend school. Managing finances can become time-consuming with the absence of the appropriate software. Software is a means of illuminating paperwork that is stored away in files and folders. Going through files and folders for specific financial data could be tedious and frustrating, especially when things are not in order. Alternatively, purchasing a computer with the appropriate financial software would definitely be the right thing to do. This will enable you to have information at hand in record time, and would ultimately bring peace of mind and satisfaction when managing your finances.

4. Financial Goals

Discussing major financial goals that you want to meet as a couple, such as buying a car, should be done at a time that is convenient to both husband and wife. So often money matters are discussed at the most inappropriate time and place (such as in church, in the store, or in front of others) and no good solutions are reached.

Husbands and wives need to be in a relaxed atmosphere, having their notepads and pens ready to discuss and document. This approach will save time and procrastination when it comes to planning.

5. Dealing with Accounts

Some husbands and wives prefer to have separate bank accounts. If either party has a business, it is highly recommended to have a separate account. Many years ago, I fell short regarding my Internal Revenue Service taxes for my business, in the amount of $25,000. The IRS wasted no time to come after my real estate and bank account to garnish the same. Fortunately, they found out that one of my clients had a balance due of $25,500 for services that were rendered by my company. They pursued that $25,500.00 and after receiving it, I was notified by mail and enclosed was a check for the $500 that remained. Personal accounts cannot be joined with business since they are two different entities. Nevertheless, a joint account is essential to build trust, love, and friendship in marriage. A joint account enhances the relationship. Not only are the finances pooled, but also the hearts are joined. At a very early stage of our marriage, my wife and I saw the need for a joint account. To date it's going strong as ever, and there has never been an issue of unfaithfulness or otherwise; though we have individual accounts with minimal funds, we are very supportive of each other's financial goals, as well as our goals as husband and wife.

6. Financial Transparency

It's paramount for a long-lasting relationship in marriage. Financial infidelity literally drives thousands of couples to the divorce courts on a daily basis. Couples like to know that their hard-earned money is secured into an honest relationship. In some cases, wives are completely untrustworthy. They sometimes go an extra mile to give their parent or some good friend money to put away for them. In terms of creating a secret account or getting involved in a monthly or weekly pool (Susu), this kind of behavior creates barriers between husbands and wives that could subsequently lead to divorce.

Her money and his money should be known to each party. Her money is money that belongs to the wife exclusively. Money that was earned by her or given to her by her husband was as a result of her labor. That money (her money) should be utilized to do whatever pleases her. Her husband has no jurisdiction over her spending or sharing. That money becomes her personal possession. If she feels like going to the restaurant, purchasing six pairs of shoes at once, giving a friend $500...that's her business. The husband has the right to exercise all of his rights when it comes to spending his money. Unfortunately, there are relationships where the wife wants to be in control of everything. Subsequently, the divorce court intervenes.

One of the greatest enemies that stand between the finances of a husband and wife is credit card debt. Many couples go into a marriage without being aware of the debt of their spouses. After entering into a supposedly long-lasting relationship, the hidden baggage of financial burden begins to manifest or be revealed. Poor handling of credit cards is a natural hindrance to a thriving relationship. These problems should be dealt with seriously and expeditiously to save the union. There are couples who take a portion of the wedding vow that says, "For better or worse, for richer or poorer" out of context. To say that vow is self-explanatory, when being caught in credit card expenses.

7. Getting out of Financial Debt

One of the greatest temptations in our world today is money. History has proven that the poor, rich, and famous have been tempted to have more than enough, and are willing to do almost anything or go the extra mile to establish their goal or target of money. There is nothing wrong with earning more money. But the Bible warns us the love of money is the root of all evil.

The root causes for anyone to be in financial debt are poor management, unemployment, making bad financial decisions, excessive spending, and lack of tithing—the genesis of debt being a habit of not having any regards for the value of money or money management. This habit swiftly develops into an addiction that trains the mind and the hand to coordinate spending money in the most radical and unthinkable ways.

This habit is prevalent in the teenager's culture. The main culprit or medium that this habit of spending is being manifested or channeled through is the credit card companies. Statistics tell us more than 60 percent of teenagers are being caught up in credit card debt yearly. This is a common assault even in relationships between husband and wife. This is one of the reasons why so many marriages are on the verge of divorce and recovery.

This subtle habit was probably initiated by what should have been considered junk mail in most cases, requesting pertinent information that will enable you to receive instant credit of literally thousands of dollars. Who would want to miss out on this so-called American dream? After all, there is nothing more exciting than financial freedom, especially for our teenage boys and girls. This is just a natural phenomenon. The merchants know how to attract them. They literally studied their minds and how they function.

If our teenagers can change name-brand sneakers or clothing every day, they will view that as cool, calm, and collected. They like to be in competition, just living for today and forgetting about tomorrow. They are never ready, however, to take responsibility for their own actions. I taught my teenagers long ago that there will always be consequences for whenever bad decisions are made in our lives.

Our teenagers utilize their credit card to fulfill their financial responsibilities in cases of clothing bills, party bills, food bills, college bills, and the list goes on...The truth of the matter is, before they are ready for college, they declare broke, simply because most of our teenagers do not have a source of a substantial income to pay their credit card balance or expenses. Credit card debts are like a burden or weight that sits on your head and follows you wherever you go. It's provocative and obnoxious.

Prior to the final stages of a relationship (entering into a union), both parties should endeavor to get out of financial debt by all means necessary. I have known husbands and wives who sank deep into financial debt because of mismanagement of their money and excessive use of their credit cards. This subsequently put a severe dent in their credit. And so for them to endure, they began to utilize their children's social security numbers to establish new credit.

Financial debt will bring us into a state of discombobulation; it has the ability to dislocate our minds, which will bring us into a state of being unbalanced. God wants us to be balanced in whatever is our engagement. If we are unbalanced, it means that we are not focusing and that we are losing sight of the things that God wants us to do and to be. The world system has set up traps for us from a tender age, and to keep us in bondage if we are not careful for the rest of our lives.

Every adult and teenager should avoid credit cards as much as possible. Here are some hints to remember:

1. Do cash deals if possible.
2. Keep only one credit card for emergencies.
3. Evaluate your spending on a regular basis.
4. Remember, money has wings when used carelessly.
5. Avoid buying excessive footwear, clothing, and anything you will not be using on a regular basis.
6. Remember you have one body, not several.

Personal testimony:

I counseled my teenagers every day on the subject of money management and credit card dilemmas, because I have passed through the ranks of poor money management and credit card debt. Years ago, I was the proud owner of six credit cards, which swiftly led me into financial lack. I was very embarrassed at that time. But to me it was a life lesson that taught me something about debt that I will always remember. That is, anyone can get into debt in seconds, but getting out of debt can take several years. It's like putting on extra weight happens so quickly; to take off that same weight can be a lifetime job if you are careless.

My children are fascinated with name-brand sneakers, name-brand clothing, and the latest hairstyle, which cost hundreds of dollars. But thanks be to God, I am not the kind of father who dishes out money and gives them whatever pleases them, but rather my wife and I will get together and make conscious decisions that will help us to spend wisely and at the same time do justice to our children.

I am challenging every parent or guardian to take a stand with me to set a precedent in your family by helping your children to control their spending habits.

This will alleviate pitfalls in their future, regardless if they are single or married.

One of the best ways to clear off credit cards debt and to avoid collection agencies is by planning your monthly expenses and budgeting an amount each month to pay off your debt. It's a win-win game when it comes to credit card expenses. If the wife is broke, the husband is broke also. Vice versa, for God's words declare that the two shall be one.

3 John 1:2 declares that above all, God wants us to be prosperous in all things and be in good health even as our soul prospers. The scripture also said, "A good man shall leave an inheritance for his children's children." Proverbs 13:22

9

Sexual Pleasure in Marriage

God's purpose for sexual pleasure in marriage is for procreation. Genesis 1:27b tells us that God created male and female, not male and male. He instructed them to be fruitful and multiply. Fill the earth and subdue it...God intended a sinless Adam and Eve to have children and "increase in number." Human sexuality was invented by God himself, and is intended as a gift within the framework of marriage. Sexual expression is a joyful affirmation of a couple's intimacy, and every pleasure is blessed by God himself. What guidelines can we use to improve our sexual intimacy?

First, whether we are newly married or have years of experience, we need to know that this relationship will require patience, understanding, and a willingness to communicate together about this sacred aspect of our marriage. It will require frequent monitoring and evaluation, because there must be a sharing of our own sexual feelings, preferences, and responses. Sexual intimacy, after all, is a new venture for brides and grooms who will need to cooperate, assist, and provide gentle, clear instruction to each other. Remember, no man is an island. We must be good teachers and humble students, for we must learn together. As the life cycle adds years, the complexities of our lives and physical changes may affect our sexual responses. Feelings and reactions are usually different during pregnancy, after childbirth, or in our later years. Sexual interest is not always static. Aging may affect hormonal levels. We may need more time for sexual arousal, or more physical stimulation for arousal—but there is no reason why healthy individuals should not find satisfaction in their sexual relations their entire lives.

Second, it is clear that sexual fulfillment begins with the quality of life in the nonsexual areas of marriage. It is difficult for either spouse to give freely and fully, without fear of being hurt, when the companion is upset, angry, or moody. The sexual expression is a barometer of a couple's total marriage experience. Dating and courting—in marriage—should be a stepping stone for a lifelong experience in marriage if faithfulness prevails during this period. Spouses need to set boundaries in advance. Talking frequently about the importance of caring and sharing in this respect can somehow have an indelible effect in the relationship, for heightened sexual pleasure and intimacy.

Third, in general, men may have a greater interest in sex because orgasm is more predictable for them. Statistics tell us that men imagine more sexual pictures than women. If that is true in your marriage (and in some marriages the woman would like more intimacy than the husband), it will require mutual understanding. A husband will need to exercise self-control, restraint, charity, and sensitivity in meeting his wife's needs, desires, and interests. On the other hand, it is validating to a husband when a wife initiates this time together. Charity must always be the ruling virtue for both. Mutual consideration will allow each spouse to be comfortable in initiating intimate contact and realizing there are occasions when sexual relations ought to be deferred. Knowing that husbands are sexually aroused by erotic messages and that women enjoy a romantic approach is important for both to understand. Of course, holding and touching, and genuine expressions of love and endearment are important elements for both.

Fourth, both spouses should be aware that a number of factors may hinder their sexual satisfaction. If either one is unsympathetic to the pressures and worries of the spouse, or if physical factors interfere— weight, hygiene, poor technique, verbal abuse, lack of forgiveness, cultural differences—may detract from their responses. There will be times when neither spouse feels "sexy," or sexually aroused. Both will need to be mature enough to realize there are no performance standards, no one to please except each other. Both must share their own honest feelings about sexual pleasure, realizing that respect and love for each may override personal preferences at times.

Fifth, because of strong premarital sexual standards and premarital abstinence for some partners, married couples may not be quite sure of how to be loving partners. Each must realize that the best source of help is the companion. The spouse is the one who can best provide feedback and instruction on sexual technique. Some couples go for years without sharing how they would prefer to be loved. A sincere desire to learn and please each other, coupled with a sense of humor— neither one embarrassing the other—can do much to increase sexual fulfillment. Both must help each other to an arousal of sexual passion and be interested in the spouse's sexual satisfaction. This sometimes can be painful, especially for the wives, when the husbands experience an early ejaculation and his partner is not properly aroused, moreover, to experience fulfillment.

Sixth, marriage is not just for sexual relations, of course, but it is a profound means of expressing love and commitment. The Bible says, "marriage is honorable and the bed is undefiled." It is designed to be a physical, emotional, and spiritual union, hence a form of marital "validation." Just as a good marriage increases sexual interest, so satisfactory sexual relations foster soul-binding emotional strength to the marriage. There are ways as powerful as the sexual union of a man and woman that are so expressive of mutual love. In shutting out the world, a couple, in the privacy of their own space, renews mutual commitments. Feelings of love and appreciation, a willingness to cooperate, to share in the joys and challenges of mortality, to be therapeutic, are sown in the sacred union of a couple whose love is centered in charity and eternal covenants.

Both can be raised to a greater level of spirituality by an act of love that expresses their emotional feelings so aptly. I have seen couples who have gone years without sharing sexual intimacy. What a tremendous loss it has been to their souls. How consoling, how refreshing, how relaxing and wholesome physical intimacy should be for couples who live in a world of stress, and who are in need of frequent reassurance that they are desirable and loved by their eternal companion. When we meet each other's sexual needs, trust is strengthened and our ability to function as a team increases. Our relationship is eternal. That means we can afford to be patient with our sexual feelings before marriage, and we can be patient with our sexual progress and the processes that will develop between the two of us.

The media myth of the perfect (and instant) orgasm is just that—a myth. In most marriages, it will take some time before a couple can establish the psychological and emotional climate where our expression of love for each other ripens and matures. So much stress in our society is put on the mechanics, techniques, and skills of intimate contact that it is easy to view a sexual encounter as an athletic performance! It's not a game and no one should be keeping score. Another gentle reminder is that you're in this together for the long haul. No one has a problem alone. If the husband is troubled with sexual difficulties, it is a problem for both companions. If a wife is unable to respond well to romantic and sexual stimuli, the problem can best be solved by both partners.

The sexual relationship is part of the total relationship. The husband who treats his wife with little respect is not likely to find a warm reception when he sends out affectionate signals after an evening of insensitive treatment of his wife! Sexual signals should not begin in the bed. The bed is likened to the stage, a place for the real performance. Both parties should learn to arouse each other during the course of the day, by the things they do, say, and even give to each other. This would definitely build up a greater level of sexual interest. Based upon my own experience when it comes to sexual pleasure, some of the worst times to approach your spouse are whenever she had a bad day at work, with the children, or even worse, an unsettled quarrel with you. If you want mama to dance, you have to play the right music. Here are some simple reminders:

1. Develop a vocabulary so that you can discuss intimacy comfortably—and often.

2. As you discover what pleases you and what you enjoy—share that with your spouse. It's your responsibility to assist your companion in meeting your needs—after all, you are the expert on you. You may wish that your partner could read your mind and your body—and eventually, in a good sexual relationship, you will be so in tune with each other that you may be able to, but that will probably come much later.

3. Learn what constitutes a good experience for your partner. It means that you must learn from your spouse about moods, timing, and what is relaxing, stimulating, and pleasurable. Both of you should be able to answer these questions: What situations make lovemaking the best experience for me? For you? What is really needed and wanted in the way of techniques for me? For you? What aspects of lovemaking are the most pleasurable for me? For you? What about frequency? Environment? And even if I know what the answers have been in the past, how about this time? Phrases such as, "I really enjoy it when you…" or "How do you feel about…" Phrases such as, "I really enjoy it when you…" or "How do you feel about…" or, "I think the thing I enjoy most about our intimacy is…" may help.

4. For "old marriages," part of the process is realizing that a series of steps exist between the first physical touch and the most passionate embrace. What are those steps in your marriage? Some couples tend to skip these steps after they have been married for a while and focus only on the final stages of sexual expression. Generally the greatest tenderness and romance are expressed either before or after our intimate time together.

10

Dealing with Barriers in Marriage

Barriers in marriages will have an indelible effect on the relationship that could lead to divorce if they continue over a period of time. Most barriers, however, are a result of selfishness, pride, and a broken covenant from either of the spouses. In addition, we all face specific barriers that hinder a deepening communication in our marriages. First, we all carry some baggage with us from our upbringing. Probably the neighborhood where we were raised was not people-friendly. We were raised in a friendless atmosphere. Our parents may have never communicated with each other or with us. They may have told us that children are to be seen and not heard. The background of parents has a lot to do with the way children are being raised. This could impact a child's life negatively or positively from childhood to adulthood. Second, we live in an isolating culture. Things like television, the Internet, and video games isolate us from those nearest and dearest to us. We get comfortable finding our own meaning, purpose, and values without having to interact and communicate with others. Third, we are bombarded with outside and inside pressures. Jobs, carpools, church meetings, housekeeping, school, helping our children with their homework, doing groceries, and the like, can steal the quality time needed for real communication between husbands and wives. Fourth, we tend to be lazy, gravitating to the nearest comfort zone. The bed takes the place of our spouse's arm. Real marital communication takes time, effort, understanding, trust, and planning. It is not for the fainthearted. And fifth, we may be fearful of showing our emotions or of being rejected if we communicate openly and honestly.

Personal Testimony

My wife and I had a brief period of struggles with culture barriers after we said, "I do." I was born and raised in Guyana, South America, and my wife was born and raised in Jamaica, West Indies. Some of our barriers were based upon the utensils we eat from. My wife feels comfortable giving me soup in a Tupperware bowl; I was feeling completely the opposite, very uncomfortable. Culturally speaking, my mother gives me soup in a stoneware bowl. I was not comfortable eating out of a Tupperware bowl; this of course motivates the tongue to pour out callous words. My wife loves flowers. I prefer to give something that has lasting value. Flowers would last her for a short time, but a plant would last her for many years. Nevertheless, the Lord had it so that after a while, both of us realized that what we were doing was stupid and childish. We recognized that it was time for marital maturity. We began to pray for it and the good Lord graciously granted it unto us. Today we are proud of each other, and we love each other dearly, all because of God's amazing grace.

Recommendations to Alleviate Barriers in Marriage

1. Seek God for your bone and flesh (Gen. 2:23)

Potential couples should seek the Lord through praying and fasting for specific answers from the Lord himself. They should not allow themselves to make anxious decisions based upon the person's physical attributes, because what you see is not always what you get. Take into consideration that your decision can either make or break you. Don't let your friends' or relatives' decisions guide you. There is nothing wrong with listening to people's opinions, but you need to hear from God for yourself. One of the biggest mistakes young people make is listening to their friends and allowing their decisions to be based on what their friends think.

If you make a mistake based on your friend's decision, your friend has nothing to lose, but you have everything to lose. I am a testimony to this test. I included God's guidance in my pursuit for a wife. On several occasions I was told that she was not the right one for me, but I did not made my choice based upon other people's opinions, but rather upon God's final answer. His answer proves to be authentic—after twenty-seven years of marriage, we are going super-great in our relationship.

2. Pursue godly and professional counseling

Every success in life is contingent upon good guidance or a coach playing an integral part in that success. When it comes to a covenant relationship, a coach should not be excluded. One of the most disappointing and disheartening things in life is to fail to plan for a lifetime. There is no guarantee that if you pursue counseling your marriage will last, but counseling gives you an opportunity to make up your mind for the journey or to back down from the journey.

A godly counselor will let you know without any uncertainty if you are stepping in the right direction or not; he will lay out to you at least one hundred things you must know before entering into a relationship that either make you or break you.

Counseling tests your readiness; it helps you to determine if you are ready or not. It tests your level of maturity. Boys and girls should not get married; marriage is for a man and a woman who understand what constitutes covenant.

Counseling tests your patience and your long-suffering. It brings out the real you. Counseling gives you the basic tools and keys to help you maintain a healthy relationship. I can recall my wife and I going to post-marital counseling once before my pastor and the board members of my church, because of a heated argument that was perpetuated by our antagonistic behavior. At the conclusion of the counseling session, my wife and I had to decide if we wanted our marriage to last or not. This was a time for serious decision making for both parties; it was an individual decision that was heading for more trouble or more peace; nevertheless, we decided to forgive each other because we recognized that both of us were acting immaturely and it wasn't justifiable.

Whenever situations and circumstances arise in marital relationships and couples find themselves before the counselors, after stating your case whether right or wrong, you have the final decision regarding the continuation of your marriage, not the counselor or coach, but you as an individual. The Bible declares in the book of Proverbs 11:14, where there is no counsel the people fall but in the multitude of counselors there is safety.

3. Counseling the parents of the bride and bridegroom

Being detached from your son or daughter can be a very painful thought. Reality is facing you, and it's not always easy to accept. The tendency of our ownership continues to linger even after being transferred to a new owner in terms of another man or woman other than your parents. Genesis 2:24 declares, "therefore, a man shall leave his mother and father, and be joined to his wife, and they shall be one flesh." God's intention in this text is that there comes a time when a man needs to leave his parents and cleave to his wife.

God is not saying that the man needs to abandon his parents, but rather he needs to assume the greater level of responsibility toward his flesh and bones (Gen. 2:23). The Bible clearly states that when a man finds a wife, he's found a good thing (Prov. 18:22). To level the playing field among the man and his wife, and their parents, both godly and professional counseling will be required. The counselor should establish boundaries for the parents of the bride and groom. They will be reminded not to interfere with every aspect of their children's relationship.

Most parents like to advise the children what to do in critical moments when there is a crisis in the relationship, inasmuch as they find themselves taking sides. This attitude can ruin the relationship, especially if either parent did not agree for their child to be married. The counselor should point out the presence of the couple and give the parents the do's and don'ts. He will also deal with the danger of carrying baggage into your marriage.

4. Avoid baggage in your relationship

Carrying baggage into your relationship is like transferring bad habits from one location to the next. The term "baggage" is simply used to define bad habits that a person develops over a period of time that may lead to addictions. Baggage brings about sour relationships and can hinder a healthy relationship from moving to the next level. No one wants to hear about your past, especially if it was a terrible past. Imagine telling your wife that you were a pervert or you *used* to be gay. It would take a portion of love for the Lord to stay with you.

The past destroys trust and confidence. It weakens your commitment and comfort. Your husband or wife should avoid at all costs bringing the past into the present. Avoid bringing your parents' current situation into your relationship. It can not only disturb your relationship with your spouse, it can destroy it.

Of course, you should ensure all debts have been paid off before seriously considering a relationship. Renounce all intimate relationships you had prior to your potential wife or husband. You need to do a checklist to ensure that all previous baggage is nullified before pursuing a serious intimate relationship.

11

Parental Role
in Marriage

The parental role in marriage pictures a farmer and a plant. It begins with sowing a seed and reaping the fruit of your labor. Raising children in the twenty-first century is somewhat different from that of ancient times. In ancient times there were far fewer divorces and more commitment and stability in the union, compared to today's society. Modern parents are willing to settle for a quick fix in their relationship. They are willing to give the relationship a try, with the hope of quitting if it does not work. The length of their relationship is contingent upon their behavior, forbearance of each other, the span of their tolerance, and the list goes on.

In the ancient times, the determined factor and the length of a union were built on love, trust, and respect for each other. The parental role in marriage depends heavily on the parents' interaction with each other, since they have an awesome responsibility to be their children's role models, counselors, and coaches until they pass or survive the worst.

Having a new member in the family is typically an exciting, welcoming event. Very often, the transition from non-parent to parent is a very stressful one. Responsibilities change overnight and never change back to the way they were prior to a child. Many factors can influence how a new baby impacts the parental role in marriage, whether it is the first child or not. These factors sometimes influence their decisions. For example, they consider job security or career levels. Some husbands or wives have financial goals they would like to reach prior to having a child. They may also consider the level of their maturity or readiness, which can have an indelible effect on the relationship. A well-balanced preparation is paramount.

The first baby will have a large impact on the husband and wife's routine, since the couple only had themselves to worry about before the baby. The baby came on board with an extra mouth that demands food, and an extra body and personality that demand attention from the parents. Because of the child's complexity, with time and experience, parents learn to adjust and to address the most critical condition or crises that might come up.

Mothers and fathers may differ in some of the ways they accommodate a new infant. On the average, mothers are much more attached to their babies than the fathers. Mothers respond more frequently to their baby's signal and learn the baby's needs. They understand what it means to carry a child for nine months, then give birth to that child in the midst of excruciating pain. Mothers are nurturers; for this reason they cannot resist the cry of their infant. In most instances mothers associate their baby's cry with the pain they felt giving birth. Crying is a language that good mothers understand, but tears are certainly a language that God understands.

Most mothers create a bond with their infant very early after birth. My wife would put her baby next to her in the bed to sleep, rather than putting the baby in a crib that is isolated from her. She gave the baby a sense of security, and at the same time was very protective. I can remember when my wife gave birth to our first child; she would literally walk around the house with the child in her hands. Whenever she was taking a shower, she would ensure that her baby was in the bathroom with her.

Some fathers, however, are more likely to disregard signals and direct the baby's attention to other things. Their tolerance level of the crying baby is much lower, since they continue their leisure activity, such as watching a sport or reading their newspaper while the baby is yearning for their attention by doing what they know best (crying). Strange to say, I was not a typical father when my wife gave birth to our first child. I was very protective and caring; I would do everything in my power to prevent my child from falling. I would literally keep watch on my baby all day. During the night, however, our baby provided a certain amount of stress on both of us. It became imperative for us to provide food periodically during the night.

Social support: This plays an important role in a child's upbringing. This support may come from grandparents or other family members who have years of experience in this area. Titus 2:3-8 has laid responsibilities upon the pastors to remind the older women in the congregation, rather than to be poor in behavior and be slanderers, some of their duties are to teach the younger women in the body of Christ and in their communities how to take care of their husbands. Likewise, the older men should be sober, reverent, temperate, sound in faith, in love, and in patience, and to exhort the young men to be sober-minded, in all things showing themselves to be a pattern of good works; in doctrine showing integrity, reverence, incorruptibility, and sound speech that cannot be condemned.

Using a social network helps parents not to be isolated, but rather develop parental skills. In addition, they are often able to help identify and understand child-rearing problems. My wife's niece recently gave birth to her first child, but was naive regarding the fundamental responsibilities of child rearing. Because of my wife's years of child-rearing experiences, she was able to communicate the right approach towards taking care of her baby's skin, his regular exercising, food, her breast, and other basic child care. Social support alleviates unnecessary sickness, viruses, and other possible discomforts.

Creating the right atmosphere: Both parents are responsible for creating an atmosphere that is comfortable for their children. The parent's personality will determine the kind of atmosphere. If either parent is selfish towards the baby, a poor atmosphere is inevitable. Children need to be raised in an atmosphere that is not hostile, but rather loving and caring, because children live what they learn. Learning has to do with seeing, hearing, touching...what a child sees, hears, and touches may have a lasting effect on the child's life. The child's behavior is molded by their parent's example: The child models after their parent; their parent is their first teacher that will impact their lives.

If you want to raise a smoker, all you have to do is to practice smoking before your child. If you want raise an alcoholic, all you have to do is practice drinking before your child.

Education: Education should begin from the womb. Great mothers begin communicating with their children from the womb. After giving birth, they develop a bond by constantly talking, laughing, and reading with their baby. Fathers teach them to say da da. Both parents are responsible for their children's education. As the child advances in age, the nature of education changes. Education is progressive and not regressive. Parents need to educate their child on the basis of God's word, apart from academia. Philosopher John Dewy said, "Education is necessary for social reform" and, "education proceeds all times/everywhere." Likewise, philosopher Quintillion said, "The cornerstone of education must be set in the earliest years." He stresses work, play, writing, and reading, but not too much mathematics." Choices: Teaching your child to make good choices from a tender age is important from a biblical perspective. Choices consist of that mental process of thinking, involved in judging the merits of multiple options and selecting one for action. Simple examples can involve choosing goodness or wickedness in personal behavior. Our world today is full of diverse kinds of influences that can easily contaminate your child or children, in spite of their age group. Teaching your child to make good choices from an early age will have a definitive effect on him or her as they grow older.

Society has taught us to be like the Joneses, regardless of what it takes to dress like them, drive like them, and live like them. But wisdom has taught us to look in the other direction because fads last only for a time and season. Parents are responsible to teach their children to be selective. Selection has to do with right and wrong, with quality over quantity, with worth instead of value.

Deception of some music: Hip-hop music has a greater impact on our teenager's mind than the good old Gospel music. Our teenagers prefer to spend hours listening to Alicia Keys, 50 Cent, and other hip-hop superstars rather than to listen to BeBe Winans or Kirk Franklin gospel CDs...They are more fascinated with the hip-hop artists than the Gospel artists. Christian parents have an awesome responsibility to instill in their children's mind what the word of God says concerning the subject of music.

The subject of music would be simple if it were not for another plan devised and skillfully implemented by an enemy of God's children—the great deceiver. He purposely twisted everything in the world and the church to his evil end.

His twisted lyrics promise delight, but bring anguish; they appear to be innocent, but are masterpieces of deception. They claim to be true but are lies. The children of God are surrounded by two aligning plans: the lyrics of the music and the cunning composer of the lyrics. Nothing is as easy and simple as it may first appear.

The early church approached the use of music with caution, aware of both its dangers and its potential. They assimilated and summarized music as follows: Music was expected to serve the glorification of God and edification of man. Music was regarded as one of the best teachers available for both good and bad. Music required and received vigilance by church authorities, and concerns were addressed decisively by modifying the practice of the church. These concerns have much to say also about the church's music practice today.

Another aspect of choice that parents need to cultivate in their children is the different type of TV and video programs they permit their children to watch. Most parents who are grounded in the word of God instill a sense of morals in the choices their children make. They do not have to be like a watchdog to evaluate the kind of images their children are being entertained by on the television, in videos, or even on the Internet.

Ah, the Internet...our society is being populated with perverts and Internet hackers, who are constantly awaiting children who, for some reason, find themselves on the wrong turf at the wrong time. Parents who spend quality time in teaching their children to make good choices will certainly minimize and eventually eliminate failures in some of the most important areas of their lives; subsequently, they will not have to face cruel consequences. There are consequences in choices.

12

Blessings and Benefits of Equal Yoke in Marriage

God, who is blessed, ordained marriage. History tells us that the first two persons to get married in the Bible were Adam and Eve. There are two outstanding qualities in this union, one consistent of Adam the man and Eve the woman. The Bible is clear on the theory that God created Adam and Eve and not Adam and Steve. The second outstanding quality in their union was the ability to reproduce. God created man and woman with reproductive organs so that they could reproduce their own kind.

The term "equally yoked" is defined as being compatible in character, religion, tastes, likes, and dislikes, but not in terms of gender. It means to be well matched, like-minded, and similar in temperament and well suited. If spouses are not compatible, the relationship is likely to have problems. Compatibility is a sign of a good relationship and a long-lasting marriage. There are no shortcuts in an unequal yoke. God in his words refuted this concept because of disunity in a union, which was designed by God Almighty to be an unbroken covenant between a man and a woman.

In 2 Corinthians 6, Paul urges the brethren not to be unequally yoked with unbelievers. He asked a profound question: For what fellowship hath righteousness with unrighteousness? And what communion hath light with darkness? Paul's contrast of righteousness with unrighteousness and darkness with light is prevalent in Christendom today. This is the reason there are more divorces in the church than in the world. It's indeed a sad commentary to think about. He proceeded by pointing out some of the dangers that will surface in an unequally yoked relationship.

Righteousness is likened unto God, and unrighteous is likened unto Satan. The Bible tells us that Satan is the enemy of God; likewise, if you are righteous and your spouse is unrighteous you both would be enemies. God wants us to live to enjoy his blessings of peace and happiness, not hatred and pain. Light and darkness are not compatible. Paul said they will not enjoy communion with each other. For light represents Jesus and darkness is a representation of Satan. Try to walk in the dark and you will stumble, as opposed to walking in the light where your path would be safe.

I have known of numerous couples who have gone into relationships that were totally incompatible. As a result, the consequences were severe and for many years affected both the spouses and the children. I have known of cases that involved the wife, husband, and three children. The husband remarried, got his new wife pregnant, but still saw his first wife and children. When his second wife realized the game that he was playing with both women, she was very disturbed; she consequently asked him for a divorce. He refused the proposal. Subsequently, his children were caught into the rat race, though they were innocent. Currently, they are literally suffering from damaging emotions. They don't know what to believe.

There are children who are suffering in our world today from broken relationships, and are not enjoying the blessings and benefits from being equally yoked in marriage. We have a responsibility to create an oasis of peace and tranquility in our homes and then in society. To accomplish this task we must, however, seek the most appropriate place (the altar) to ask God to direct us to his will and choice in choosing a spouse.

There is a right one for everyone who passes through God's channel of choosing. There are also consequences in making the wrong choice in choosing a mate. Here are five criteria I recommend using when choosing for compatibility (equally yoked) from a Christian perspective.

1) He or she must be a Christian man or woman who was raised preferably in the same denomination. This would help to minimize doctrinal fights, thus controlling the temperature in the relationship. Denominational barriers can create a lifetime of misery for both parties. The fact remains that if one party grew up Catholic faith and the other grew up as an Adventist, that will cause disparity in the union, since one party wants to go to church on Sunday and the other wants to go on Saturday.

The word "gratum" comes from the Latin word "agreed," which translates the neuter of "gratus," pleasing, agreeable, to get along together, or to be similar. Unless there is some degree of mutual understanding, peace will not be possible in the relationship. The Bible defended this man-made selfish theory in the book of Amos 3:3: "Can two walk together, except they are agreed?"

God wants harmony and fellowship in every relationship. He smiles when husbands and wives can do things together. It pictures the triune God (the Godhead); there is unity in a relationship that is balanced.

2) They should be good communicators. Communication plays an integral part in every relationship; therefore, both parties must strive to improve their communication skills at all times. Poor communication skills contribute to more than 50 percent of divorces in the church. It's amazing to see how most relationships begin with excitement, and suddenly come to an end. Both parties are responsible to be good listeners during the communication process. They must learn the skills to be the sender and the receiver simultaneously. Because communication is a complex process, it takes time to comprehend.

Comprehension depends upon many factors, for example, one's background. How you were raised, where you were raised, cultural differences, language barriers, hobbies, training, what was your parents' lifestyle, and a whole host of other factors can have some degree of impact on the way you communicate. Nevertheless, you should communicate ultimately for harmony in the relationship.

3) Possessors of good character: There is nothing more awesome than good character in a union. Good character breeds an avenue for complementation. Character refers to one being capable of portraying an unusual personality that commands attention. People are drawn to husbands and wives who are focused in a similar area for a common good. For instance, in a church setting where there are married couples, people are constantly looking for someone who they can confide in. They look for couples that have similar personalities, temperament, and a godly disposition to confide in.

People with character are destined to higher heights and deeper depths. They are destined to success in all phases of life, because character speaks of one's inner spirit. It envelops the whole person in terms of behavior, morality, and trustworthiness. Having a good character will take you to places you have never been before. It's not a thing of the past, but of the present and future. This has a direct link to blessing and benefit in a marital experience, especially when the union is equally yoked. Likewise, lack of character drives sinners into your path, for two negatives remain negative.

Poor self-esteem can be a direct barrier to good character. It starves the inner you from being motivated to higher heights and greater depths. The antidote to conquer low self-esteem is for you to realize that God loves you; regardless of what man thinks about you, God still loves you. Husbands and wives must learn to listen to their positive inner voices, and ignore the spirit of betrayal. But you can agree to disagree for a common good. Blessings and benefits from an equally yoked union can be determined by knowing what you want in the relationship. It's advisable from the pages of God's word that we pray before choosing. Many couples experience woe in their marriages because they picked their spouses first and then prayed. We want to understand that God sees the future. His words are the road map that we must use to have a safe journey. Otherwise, our journey will have potholes that we can't handle, and subsequently we will experience fatality during the course of our journey.

When I was a young convert, I was so in love with Jesus that everything else was not important. But in the process of time, during my journey, God began to prompt me to find a good thing (a wife), for the Bible teaches, "he who finds a good wife, finds a good thing." It was not long after his constant prompting that I decided what I wanted or would be looking for in a relationship. "In those days I was in love with the hymn that says, "In everything you do or say, put God first." My first step was to chart my journey with the spiritual compass, which is prayer. My prayer was specific and detailed as though I was ordering my wife from God's throne. I told him, what she must possess: "She should be a churchgoer, one who loves the Lord. Must be able to sing for the Lord, intelligent, excellent, and be a good wife and mother to our children." I had a mental picture of my wife-to-be. And so I began to process this mindset over several months by fasting and praying.

My next step was to evaluate myself to figure the compatibility between the two of us (my wife and I). I thought of cultural barriers, and the common effect this can have on our future union, because she came from a different culture. Not long after, God provided the wife that I had desired. Subsequently, I took time to examine our communication skills, strengths, and weaknesses. I also evaluated the level of our comprehension so as to maintain happiness, to prevent denominational barriers, doctrinal differences, and the "little things" that could hinder our union. I even thought of the level of mutual submission, if this could be possible or not. My brain was searching every avenue for questions and answers.

It was like standing before this imaginary woman and looking at her, and her glancing at me to ensure that everything between us matches. God knew that I was not painting a perfect or flawless woman. What mattered to me was her Christian character (doing the right thing when we know no one is watching). God knew that my heart was right, and the method of choosing a wife that was compatible and was in order. And so he sent his angels on a campaign to handpick the mental picture my mind processed for a wife. One year after meeting my wife, we got married. Thank God the union is getting stronger day by day, because it was built on the *foundation of God's love.*

Tragic to say, one of the reasons for an unequally yoked union is the theory of a woman's biological clock ticking away, and finding a man looks virtually impossible. Sad to say, women on every level buy into this misleading theory that Satan uses to betray their minds. Choosing the God kind of spouse is the foundation of a long-lasting and happy relationship. The most important component of a structure is the foundation. The foundation determines how strong the structure will be. The value of the structure is determined by the foundation. Building is used as a metaphor to give a picture of a union or the establishment of a family.

Choosing for compatibility takes quality time in prayer and fasting. The Bible tells us in the book of Ruth how Ruth met Boaz, and the procedure both of them had to go through before they were legally joined together into a union. It was not an overnight arrangement. But in the process of time, God orchestrated fellowship between the two of them, at the most unusual location (in the field). This story gives us a sense of trust in God for our future spouse.

In today's generation, the enemy uses unfaithfulness to establish unequally yoked relationships. That is to say, if a young Christian girl got pregnant out of wedlock, to avoid shame, the parents of the girl and boy would get together and agree to marry them even before the pregnancy was matured or visible. This type of mentality creates premature unions with immature couples. Lack of maturity in a relationship is like babies wearing booties and Pampers. They don't know right from wrong. This behavior has become very prevalent in our society over the years.

There is a breakdown in the value system. We need to better understand who we are and whose we are as God's people before we can fix our value system. Values have to do with the way we evaluate ourselves before God. Ask how God sees us, in spite of the challenges of peer pressure, fads, and other circumstances that face our young Christian males and females. They need to remember that God has a standard. His standard should be excellent in all ways. They should not lower God's standard to please the self or anyone else. God should be first and foremost in their lives.

The Bible tells us to "seek God first and his righteousness" (right doings) and then all things should be added to us. All things include our spouses. God has principles, and if only we follow his principles, we will be blessed. Seek and find, knock and it shall be opened, call and he will answer. Sowing and reaping are principles that God honors since he is immutable (is not subject to change).

An unequal yoke limits the power and the manifestation of God in the home. Whenever a godly woman marries an ungodly man, the power of God is limited in the home because: (a) he is not a worshipper, (b) he refuses fellowship with God's people, (c) he does not read the Bible, and (d) in some cases he is an antichrist. The power of God's manifestation and presence is associated with an equally yoked union. Wherever there is agreement, God shows up. There is a direct link with unity and power, especially from the creations of God the Father, God the Son, and God the Holy Spirit.

www.ingramcontent.com/pod-product-compliance
Lightning Source LLC
Chambersburg PA
CBHW051549120626
46551CB00013B/1437